HOW SUCCESSFUL
PEOPLE GROW

Books by Dr. John C. Maxwell
Can Teach You How to Be a REAL Success

Relationships

25 Ways to Win with People

Becoming a Person of Influence

Encouragement Changes Everything

Ethics 101

Everyone Communicates, Few Connect

The Power of Partnership

Relationships 101

Winning with People

Attitude

Attitude 101

The Difference Maker

Failing Forward

How Successful People Think

Sometimes You Win— Sometimes You Learn

Success 101

Thinking for a Change

The Winning Attitude

Equipping

The 15 Invaluable Laws of Growth

The 17 Essential Qualities of a Team Player

The 17 Indisputable Laws of Teamwork

Developing the Leaders Around You

Equipping 101

Make Today Count

Mentoring 101

My Dream Map

Partners in Prayer

Put Your Dream to the Test

Running with the Giants

Talent Is Never Enough

Today Matters

Your Road Map for Success

Leadership

The 10th Anniversary Edition of The 21 Irrefutable Laws of Leadership

The 21 Indispensable Qualities of a Leader

The 21 Most Powerful Minutes in a Leader's Day

The 360 Degree Leader

Developing the Leader Within You

The 5 Levels of Leadership

Go for Gold

How Successful People Lead

Leadership 101

Leadership Gold

Leadership Promises for Every Day

This book is dedicated to

The team at the John Maxwell Company:
You fulfill my vision, you extend my influence,
and you make me better than I am. Your work is helping
others to maximize their potential and impact their world.

And to Curt Kampmeier, who introduced me to
the concept of intentional personal growth and in doing
so showed me the path to reaching my potential.

Contents

Acknowledgments   ix
Introduction: Growth Is the Pathway
to Your Potential   xi

1. **Become an Intentional Learner:**
   Growth Doesn't Just Happen   1

2. **Develop Self-Awareness:** You Must
   Know Yourself to Grow Yourself   9

3. **Believe in Yourself:** You Must See Value
   in Yourself to Add Value *to* Yourself   19

4. **Set Aside Time to Reflect:** Learning to
   Pause Allows Growth to Catch Up with You   29

5. **Embrace Discipline Daily:**
   Motivation Gets You Going—Discipline
   Keeps You Growing   38

6. **Seek Out a Positive Environment:**
   Growth Thrives in Conducive Surroundings   46

7. **Become Highly Strategic:**
   To Maximize Growth, Develop Strategies   56

8. **Turn Negatives into Positives:**
Good Management of Bad Experiences
Leads to Great Growth   66

9. **Grow from the Inside Out:** Character
Growth Determines the Height of
Your Personal Growth   76

10. **Get Used to Stretching Yourself:**
Growth Stops When You Lose
the Tension Between Where You Are
and Where You Could Be   86

11. **Make Smart Trade-Offs:** You Have
to Give Up to Grow Up   95

12. **Learn to Ask More Questions:**
Growth Is Stimulated by Asking *Why?*   106

13. **Find a Good Mentor:** It's Hard to
Improve When You Have No One but
Yourself to Follow   115

14. **Focus on Enlarging Your Potential:**
Growth Always Increases Your Capacity   123

15. **Help Others Reach Their Potential:**
Growing Yourself Enables You to
Grow Others   132

Acknowledgments

Thank you to:

Charlie Wetzel, my writer;

Stephanie Wetzel, my social media manager;

Linda Eggers, my executive assistant.

Introduction:
Growth Is the Pathway
to Your Potential

*P*otential is one of the most wonderful words in any language. It looks forward with optimism. It is filled with hope. It promises success. It implies fulfillment. It hints at greatness. Potential is a word based on possibilities. Think about your potential as a human being and you get excited—at least, I hope you do. What a positive thought. Do you have personal potential? Absolutely. Your personal potential is what you could be—the person you can become.

Since you are reading these words, I believe you also have the desire to reach your potential. So now the question becomes, how do you do it?

The answer is growth. And to grow, you must be highly intentional. This book is my effort to help you learn how to grow and develop yourself so you have the best chance of becoming the person you were created to be. My desire is to help you develop the right attitude, learn more about your strengths, tap into your passion, become more in touch with your purpose, and develop your skills so you can be all you can be.

What exactly do I mean when I write about growth? That

will be as unique as you are. To discover your purpose, you need to grow in self-awareness. To become a better human being, you need to grow in character. To advance in your career, you need to grow in your skills. To be a better spouse or parent, you need to grow in relationships. To reach your financial goals, you need to grow in your knowledge about how money works. To enrich your soul, you need to grow spiritually. The specifics of growth change from person to person, but the principles are the same for every person. This book offers fifteen ways for you to grow so that you can reach your potential. Each is a key that unlocks a door to a better future. You will have to put in the work to actually grow.

My recommendation is that you tackle a chapter of this book every week. Discuss it with some friends. Do the application exercises at the end of each chapter. Keep a growth journal. And incorporate what you're learning into your everyday life. You cannot change your life until you change something you do every day. If you keep learning and growing every day over the course of many years, you will be astounded by how far it will take you.

HOW SUCCESSFUL
PEOPLE GROW

1

Become an Intentional Learner
Growth Doesn't Just Happen

How do you get better at what you do? How do you improve your relationships? How do you gain more depth and wisdom as a person? How do you gain insight? How do you overcome obstacles? Work harder? Work longer? Wait for things to get better?

If you focus on goals, you may hit goals—but that doesn't guarantee growth. If you focus on growth, you will grow and always hit goals.

Growth Gap Traps

If you have dreams, goals, or aspirations, you need to grow to achieve them. But if you're like most people, you have one or more mistaken beliefs creating gaps that keep you from growing and reaching your potential. Take a look at the following eight misconceptions about growth that may be holding you back from being as intentional as you need to be.

1. The Assumption Gap—"I Assume That I Will Automatically Grow"

When we are children, our bodies grow automatically. A year goes by, and we become taller, stronger, more capable of doing new things and facing new challenges. I think many people carry into adulthood a subconscious belief that mental, spiritual, and emotional growth follows a similar pattern. Time goes by, and we simply get better. We're like Charlie Brown in Charles Schulz's *Peanuts* comic strip, who once said, "I think I've discovered the secret of life—you just hang around until you get used to it." The problem is that we don't improve by simply living. We have to be intentional about it.

No one improves by accident. Personal growth doesn't just happen on its own. And once you're done with your formal education, you must take complete ownership of the growth process, because nobody else will do it for you. If you want your life to improve, you must improve yourself. You must make that a conscious goal.

2. The Knowledge Gap—"I Don't Know How to Grow"

Many people learn only from the school of hard knocks. Difficult experiences teach them lessons "the hard way," and they change—sometimes for the better, sometimes for the worse. The lessons are random and difficult. It's much better to *plan* your growth intentionally. You decide where you need or want to grow, you choose what you will learn, and you follow through with discipline going at the pace you set.

Think about what it is that you want to do. Whom do you

want to be? Make a list of things that will help you reach that goal and be that person. Is there something on that list you can do now? Today? Do it.

When you start working actively toward your goal, you'll find that the door of personal growth opens a crack. Through that crack you'll begin to see more growth opportunities everywhere. Your world begins to open up. You accomplish more. You learn more. Other opportunities begin to present themselves.

3. The Timing Gap—"It's Not the Right Time to Begin"

Whether you feel prompted to or not, now is the time to start growing. The reality is that you will never get much done unless you go ahead and do it before you are ready. If you're not already intentionally growing, you need to get started today. If you don't, you may reach some goals, which you can celebrate, but you will eventually plateau. Once you start growing intentionally, you can keep growing and keep asking "What's next?"

4. The Mistake Gap—"I'm Afraid of Making Mistakes"

Growing can be a messy business. It means admitting you don't have the answers. It requires making mistakes. It can make you look foolish. Most people don't enjoy that. But that is the price of admission if you want to improve. If you want to grow, you need to get over any fear you may have of making mistakes. As author and professor Warren Bennis asserts, "A mistake is simply another way of doing things." To become intentional about growing, expect to make mistakes every day, and welcome them as a sign that you are moving in the right direction.

5. The Perfection Gap—"I Have to Find the Best Way Before I Start"

Similar to the Mistake Gap is the Perfection Gap, the desire to find the "best" way to get started in a growth plan. That's what I thought when I started working on my personal growth. But what I discovered is that I had it backward. I had to get started if I wanted to find the best way. It's similar to driving on an unfamiliar road at night. Ideally, you'd like to be able to see your whole route before you begin. But you see it progressively. As you move forward, a little more of the road is revealed to you. If you want to see more of the way, then get moving.

6. The Inspiration Gap—"I Don't Feel Like Doing It"

You may not feel inspired to aggressively pursue a growth plan if you haven't started yet. If that's the case, please trust me when I say that the reasons to keep growing far outweigh the reasons to start growing. And you discover the reasons to stay with growth only if you stick with it long enough to start reaping the benefits. So make a commitment to yourself to start *and* stick with it for at least twelve months. If you do, you will fall in love with the process, and you will be able to look back at the end of that year and see how far you've come.

7. The Comparison Gap—"Others Are Better Than I Am"

The first ten years that I was intentionally pursuing personal growth, I was always behind trying to catch up. I had to get over the comparison gap. I recognized I needed to be exposed to bigger and better leaders outside of my own small circle, but when

I stepped out of my comfort zone I was intimidated. It was clear that I was not in their league. Their organizations were six times the size of mine, and they had many more and much better ideas than I did. I felt like I was in over my head and trying to swim. Despite that, I was encouraged. Why? Because I discovered that great men were willing to share their ideas. And I was learning so much. You can learn only if others are ahead of you. It was a difficult transition, but it was well worth it. So if you are aware that others are better than you, don't be discouraged. Be glad others are there to help show you the way.

8. The Expectation Gap—"I Thought It Would Be Easier Than This"

I don't know any successful person who thinks growth comes quickly and climbing to the top is easy. It just doesn't happen. People create their own luck. How? Here's the formula:

Preparation (growth) + **Attitude** + **Opportunity** + **Action** (doing something about it) = **Luck**

It all starts with preparation. Unfortunately, that takes time. But here's the best news. As Jim Rohn said, "You cannot change your destination overnight, but you can change your direction overnight." If you want to reach your goals and fulfill your potential, become intentional about personal growth. It will change your life.

Making the Transition to Intentional Growth

The sooner you make the transition to becoming intentional about your personal growth, the better it will be for you, because growth compounds and accelerates if you *remain* active in pursuing it. Here's how to make the change:

1. Ask the Big Question First

The first year that I engaged in intentional personal growth, I discovered that it was going to be a lifetime process. During that year, the question in my mind changed from "How long will this take?" to "How far can I go?" That is the question you should be asking yourself right now—not that you will be able to answer it. I started this growth journey forty years ago, and I still haven't answered it. But it will help you set the *direction*, if not the distance.

> Where do you want to go in life?
> What direction do you want to go?
> What's the farthest you can imagine going?

Answering those questions will get you started on the personal-growth journey toward your potential. The best you can hope to do in life is to make the most out of whatever you've been given. You do that by investing in yourself, making yourself the best you can be. The more you've got to work with, the greater your potential—and the farther you should try to go.

2. Do It Now

The greatest danger you face in this moment is the idea that you will make intentional growth a priority *later*. Don't fall into that trap! By starting to read this book, you've already begun the process. Don't stop there! Keep taking more steps. Pick a resource that will help you grow and begin learning from it *today*.

3. Face the Fear Factor

We all have fears. But here's the good news. We also all have faith. The question you have to ask yourself is, "Which emotion will I allow to be stronger?" Your answer is important, because the stronger emotion wins. I want to encourage you to feed your faith and starve your fear.

4. Change from Incidental to Intentional Growth

People tend to get into ruts in life. They get in an easy groove, and they don't try to break out if it—even when it's taking them in the wrong direction. After a while, they just get by. If they learn something, it's because of a happy accident. Don't let that happen to you! If that is the attitude you've developed, then you would do well to remember that the only difference between a rut and a grave is the length!

If you want to reach your potential and become the person you were created to be, you must do much more than just experience life and hope that you learn what you need along the way. You must go out of your way to seize growth opportunities as if your future depended on it. Why? Because it does. Growth doesn't just happen—not for me, not for you, not for anybody. You have to go after it!

How to Become an Intentional Learner

1. Which of the Growth Gaps discussed in this chapter have caused you to neglect growing the way you perhaps could have? What strategies can you create and implement to help you bridge the gaps? Write a specific plan for each gap that applies to you and take the first step of that plan *today*.

2. Take a look at your calendar for the next twelve months. How much time have you specifically scheduled for personal growth? If you're like most people, your answer will be none. Rework your calendar so you have an appointment with yourself for personal growth every day, five days a week, fifty weeks a year. If you want to succeed, you need to do whatever it takes.

3. Start now. No matter what time of day you're reading these words, make a commitment to start growing today. Give that first hour before you go to sleep tonight. Put in the time today and for the next five days. You probably won't feel like doing it. Do it anyway.

2

Develop Self-Awareness

You Must Know Yourself to Grow Yourself

If you want to grow to your potential, you must know yourself: your strengths and weaknesses, your interests and opportunities. You must be able to gauge not only where you've been, but also where you are now. Otherwise you cannot set a course for where you want to go. And of course, every time you want to learn something, you must be able to take the new thing you've learned today and build on what you learned yesterday to keep growing. That's the only way to gain traction and keep improving yourself. Knowing yourself is like reading "You Are Here" on a map when you want to find your way to a destination.

I've observed that there are really only three kinds of people when it comes to having direction in life:

1. People Who Don't Know What They Would Like to Do

These people are often *confused*. They lack a strong sense of purpose. They don't possess a sense of direction for their lives.

If they are growing, they are unfocused about it. They dabble. They drift. They can't reach their potential because they have no idea what to shoot for. Most people seem to fall into this category. I believe the main reason is that they don't know themselves as well as they should, and thus remain unfocused in their growth.

2. People Who Know What They Would Like to Do but Don't Do It

These people are usually *frustrated*. Every day they experience the gap between where they are and where they want to be. Sometimes they aren't doing what they want because they worry that it will cause them to neglect other responsibilities, such as providing for their families. Sometimes they aren't willing to pay the price to learn, grow, and move closer to where they want to be. Other times fear prevents them from changing course to pursue their passion. No matter what the reason, they, too, miss their potential.

3. People Who Know What They Would Like to Do and Do It

The third kind of people know themselves, possess a strong sense of passion, are focused in purpose, grow in areas that help them move closer to their purpose, and do what they were created to do. The word that best describes them is *fulfilled*. Finding yourself and growing to your potential can be a bit of a catch-22. You have to know who you are to grow to your potential. But you have to grow in order to know who you are. So what's the solution? Explore yourself as you explore growth.

How to Find Your Passion and Purpose

If you want to change and grow, then you must know yourself and accept who you are before you can start building. The way to start is to pay attention to your passions. Areas that may reveal your passion and purpose include career, faith, family, communication, and creativity. Here are ten questions to help you start working through that process. These questions will help you know what to do, and also give you a sense of *how* to start moving in the right direction. They will help you to target and eventually fine-tune your growth.

1. Do You Like What You're Doing Now?

I am amazed by how many people I meet every day who don't like doing what they do for a living. Why do they do it? I understand the necessity of having to make a living. We've all done jobs we didn't love. But we don't have to stay there our whole lives, doing something we find unfulfilling. Is it a risk making a change from what you're currently doing to what you *want* to do? Of course. You might fail. You might find out that you don't like it as much as you expected. You might not make as much money. But isn't there also great risk in staying where you are? You might fail. You might get fired. You might take a pay cut. Or worst of all, you might come to the end of your life feeling regret for never having reached your potential or doing what you love. Which risk would you rather live with?

2. What Would You Like to Do?

There is definitely a direct connection between finding your passion and reaching your potential. When you tap into your passion, it gives you the E&E factor: *energy* and *excellence*.

- You will never fulfill your destiny doing work you despise.
- Passion gives you an advantage over others, because one person with passion is greater than ninety-nine who have only an interest!
- Passion gives you energy.

How do you *know* what you want to do? How do you tap into your passion? Listen to your heart. Pay attention to what you love doing. If you never figure out what you want to do, you will probably be frustrated all of your life. Knowing yourself and what you want to do is one of the most important things you'll ever do in this life.

3. Can You Do What You Would Like to Do?

One of the main keys to being successful and fulfilling your purpose is to understand your unique talents and to find the right arena in which to use them. Some people have an inherent ability to know who they are and who they're not. Others have to work hard to make those discoveries. Your goal should be to waste as little of your life as possible. There's a big difference between having a dream that propels you to achieve and pulling an idea out of thin air that has no connection with who you are and what you can do. You must have some kind of criteria for knowing if the desire you have matches the abilities you possess. Measure the difference between what you want and what you're able to do, what drives you and what satisfies you, and your values and those of the organization. Are you able to overcome those differences?

4. Do You Know Why You Want to Do What You Would Like to Do?

I believe it's very important not only to know what you want to do, but also why you want to do it. I say that because motives matter. When you do things for the right reason, it gives you inner strength when things go wrong. Right motives help you to build positive relationships because they prevent hidden agendas and incline you to put people ahead of your agenda. Doing something for the right reasons also keeps life less cluttered and your path clearer. Not only is your vision clearer, but you also sleep well at night knowing you're on the right track.

5. Do You Know What to Do So You Can Do What You Want to Do?

To move from what you're doing now to what you want to do is a process. Do you know what it will take? I believe it begins with...

AWARENESS

You cannot change direction if you aren't aware that you're not headed where you want to go. Spend some time really thinking about where you're presently headed. If it's not where you want to go, then write out what steps you need to take to go where you desire to go, to do what you want to do. Make them as tangible as possible. Will they definitely be the *right* steps? Maybe, maybe not. But you won't know for sure until you start moving forward.

ACTION

You cannot win if you do not begin! The people who get ahead in the world are the ones who look for the circumstances they want, and if they can't find them, they make them. That means taking initiative. It means doing something specific every day that will take you another step closer to your goal. It means continuing to do it every day. Nearly all successes are the fruit of initiative.

ACCOUNTABILITY

Few things prompt a person to follow through like accountability. One of the ways you can do that is to make your goals public. When you tell others about what you intend to do, it puts pressure on you to keep working at it. You can request that specific individuals ask you about your progress. It's similar to having a deadline to keep you moving. You can even write things down as a form of accountability.

ATTRACTION

If you want to be around growing people, become a growing person. If you're committed, you attract others who are committed. If you're growing, you attract others who are growing. This puts you in a position to begin building a community of like-minded people who can help one another succeed.

6. Do You Know People Who Do What You'd Like to Do?

My greatest growth has always come as a result of finding people ahead of me who were able to show me the way forward. Some of them have helped me through personal contact, but most have helped through the books they've written. When I've had questions, I've found answers in their wisdom. If you have discovered what you want to do, start finding people who do what you want to do with excellence. Then do what you must to learn from them. Always remember that you cannot get where you want to go on your own. You will need the help of others to guide you on your way.

7. Should You Do What You'd Like to Do with Them?

If you are someone who is dedicated to personal growth, you will always be learning from many people in many places. Occasionally you will have an opportunity to be mentored on an ongoing basis by an individual. Being mentored by someone who is successful in your area of interest has great value, and I will discuss it more thoroughly in the chapter on finding a mentor. But remember, every person who *can* help you is not necessarily the right person *to* help you. You must pick and choose. And so must they. Your goal should be to find a fit that is mutually beneficial for both mentor and mentee.

8. Will You Pay the Price to Do What You Want to Do?

When it comes to barriers to success, we are usually our own worst enemies. Taking the steps necessary to live your dreams and do what you want to do will cost you. You will have to work hard. You will have to make sacrifices. You will have to keep learning and growing and changing. Are you willing to pay that price? I certainly hope you are. But know this: Most people aren't.

9. When Can You Start Doing What You'd Like to Do?

Ask people when they will do what they want to do, and most answer that they hope to do it "someday." Why not now? Because you're not ready? Perhaps you're not. But if you wait until you are, maybe you never will do it. You only get ready by starting.

10. What Will It Be Like When You Get to Do What You'd Like to Do?

Because I've had the privilege of doing what I've always wanted to do, I want to help you see ahead to what it's like.

It will be *different* from what you imagined. I never thought that I would affect as many people as I do. I never knew life would be so beautiful. I never thought I would occasionally want to withdraw from people to think and write. But I also never anticipated the expectations others would put on me to produce.

It will be *more difficult* than you ever imagined. I had no idea how much time it would take to be effective. I never expected to have such great demands put on my life or to have to keep paying the price to be successful. I also never dreamed that my energy level would go down as much as it has in recent years.

Finally, it will be *better* than you ever imagined. When I started investing in my personal growth, I didn't anticipate a compounding return—for me personally, for the individuals I've mentored, and for my team. And I never dreamed it would be this much fun! Nothing else compares to doing what you were created to do.

People say there are two great days in a person's life: the day you were born and the day you discover why. I want to encourage you to seek what you were put on this earth to do. Then pursue it with all your effort.

How to Develop Self-Awareness

The questions in this chapter are designed to prompt you to know yourself and get on course to do what you were made to do in life. Here is a streamlined version of the questions. Spend a significant amount of time answering them so you will have a plan of action to follow when you're done.

1. What would you like to do?
2. What talents, skills, and opportunities do you possess that support your desire to do it?
3. What are your motives for wanting to do it?
4. What steps must you take (beginning today) to start doing what you want to do?:

   • Awareness
   • Action
   • Accountability

5. Whose advice can you get to help you along the way?
6. What price are you willing to pay? What will it cost you in time, resources, and sacrifices?
7. Where do you most need to grow? (You must focus on your strengths and overcome any weaknesses that would keep you from reaching your goal.)

3

Believe in Yourself

You Must See Value in Yourself to Add Value to Yourself

I believe all people have the seeds of success within them. All they need to do is cultivate those seeds, water them, feed them, and they will begin to grow. So why do many people fail to grow and reach their potential? I've concluded that one of the main reasons is low self-esteem. Many people don't believe in themselves. They possess a hundred acres of possibilities, yet never cultivate them because they are convinced that they won't be able to learn and grow and blossom into something wonderful.

The Power of Positive Self-Esteem

If you don't realize that you have genuine value and that you are worth investing in, then you will never put in the time and effort needed to grow to your potential. If you're not sure you agree with that, then consider the following.

Self-Esteem Is the Single Most Significant Key to a Person's Behavior

Often have I heard my friend Zig Ziglar say, "It's impossible to consistently behave in a manner inconsistent with how we see ourselves. We can do very few things in a positive way if we feel negative about ourselves." If you believe you are worthless, then you won't add value to yourself.

Low Self-Esteem Puts a Ceiling on Our Potential

If your desire is a 10 but your self-esteem is a 5, you'll never perform at the level of a 10. You'll perform as a 5 or lower. People are never able to outperform their self-image.

The Value We Place on Ourselves Is Usually the Value Others Place on Us

I'm sorry to say that most people live their lives according to what others believe about them because they accept others' value of them without question. If the important people in their lives expect them to go nowhere, then that's what they expect for themselves. That's fine if you're surrounded by people who believe in you. But what if you're not?

You shouldn't become too concerned about what others might think of you. You should be more concerned about what you think of yourself. If you put a small value on yourself, rest assured the world will not raise the price. If you want to become the person you have the potential to be, you must believe you can!

Steps to Build Your Self-Image

If self-image is a problem for you, if you don't believe you can succeed, please take to heart the following ten suggestions.

1. Guard Your Self-Talk

Whether you know it or not, you have a running conversation with yourself all the time. What is the nature of yours? Do you encourage yourself? Or do you criticize yourself? If you are positive, then you help to create a positive self-image. If you're negative, you undermine your self-worth.

If we want to change our lives, we have to change the way we think of ourselves. If we want to change the way we think of ourselves, we need to change the way we *talk* to ourselves. And the older we are, the more responsible we are for how we think, talk, and believe. Don't you have enough problems in life already? Why add to them by discouraging yourself every day with negative self-talk?

Become your own encourager, your own cheerleader. Every time you do a good job, don't just let it pass; give yourself a compliment. Every time you choose discipline over indulgence, don't tell yourself that you should have anyway; recognize how much you are helping yourself. Every time you make a mistake, don't bring up everything that's wrong with yourself; tell yourself that you're paying the price for growth and that you will learn to do better next time. Every positive thing you can say to yourself will help.

2. Stop Comparing Yourself to Others

Comparing yourself to others is really just a needless distraction. The only one you should compare yourself to is you. Your mission is to become better today than you were yesterday. You do that by focusing on what you can do today to improve and grow. Do that enough, and if you look back and compare the you of weeks, months, or years ago to the you of today, you should be greatly encouraged by your progress.

3. Move Beyond Your Limiting Beliefs

Unfortunately, a lot of people don't believe that they can accomplish great things. But the greatest limitations people experience in their lives are usually the ones they impose on themselves. For example, let's say you would like to learn a foreign language to improve your career or better enjoy a vacation, but you don't think you can do it. Once you've identified that belief, define how not learning that language is limiting you. Then describe what it will be like when you learn that language. How will it make you feel? What will it enable you to do? What might it do for your career? Then write an empowering statement that affirms your ability to learn the language, outlines the realistic process you will use to learn it, and describes how you will be impacted by this growth. Remember, in the end, it isn't what you are that holds you back; it's what you think you're not.

4. Add Value to Others

Because people with low self-esteem often see themselves as inadequate or feel like victims (which often starts because they actually have been victimized in their past), they focus inordinately on themselves. They can become self-protective and selfish because they feel that they have to be to survive.

If that is true of you, then you can combat those feelings by serving others and working to add value to them. Making a difference—even a small one—in the lives of other people lifts one's self-esteem. It's hard to feel bad about yourself when you're doing something good for someone else. In addition to that, adding value to others makes them value you more. It creates a cycle of positive feeling from one person to another.

5. Do the Right Thing, Even If It's the Hard Thing

One of the best ways to build self-esteem is to do what's right. It gives a strong sense of satisfaction. And what happens whenever you don't do the right thing? Either you feel guilt, which makes you feel bad about yourself, or you lie to yourself to try to convince yourself that your actions weren't wrong or weren't that important. That does harm to you as a person and to your self-esteem.

Being true to yourself and your values is a tremendous self-esteem builder. Every time you take action that builds your character, you become stronger as a person—the harder the task, the greater the character builder. You can actually "act yourself" into feeling good about yourself, because positive character expands into every area of your life, giving you confidence and positive feelings about everything you do.

6. Practice a Small Discipline Daily in a Specific Area of Your Life

If there is an area in your life that seems overwhelming to you—health, work, family, or something else—try chipping away at it a little bit every day instead of trying to tackle it all at once. Since your self-worth is based on the positive habits, actions, and decisions you practice every day, why not build your self-esteem and tackle your biggest problems at the same time? Don't fret or worry about it; do something specific about it. Discipline is a morale builder. Boost yours by taking small steps that will take you in a positive direction.

7. Celebrate Small Victories

This next suggestion is really a follow-up to the previous ones. When you do the right thing or you take a small step in the right direction, what is your emotional response? What kinds of things do you tell yourself? Are your thoughts like these?

> *Well, it's about time.*
> *I didn't do as much as I should have.*
> *That won't make a difference.*
> *It's hopeless—I'll never succeed.*

Or are they more like these?

> *It's good that I did that.*
> *I did the right thing—good for me!*

Every little bit helps.
I'm that much closer to success.

If your thinking runs more like the first list, then you need to change your thinking.

8. Embrace a Positive Vision for Your Life Based on What You Value

If you have a positive vision for your life and you take action to fulfill that vision, then you will more readily recognize that your life matters.

What do you value? What prompts you to see a positive vision for your life? If you don't have a vision, you are likely to be apathetic. However, if you tap into what you value and try to see what could be, it can inspire you to take positive action. And every positive action you take helps you to believe in yourself, which in turn helps you to take more positive action.

9. Practice the One-Word Strategy

A couple of years ago I read a book by Kevin Hall called *Aspire*, which really inspired me. One of my favorite passages in the book communicates something Kevin does to help people grow:

> The first thing I do when I'm coaching someone who aspires to stretch, grow, and go higher in life is to have that person select the one word that best describes him or her. Once that person does that, it's as if he or

she has turned a page in a book and highlighted one word. Instead of seeing three hundred different words on the page, the person's attention, and intention, is focused immediately on that single word, that single gift. What the individual focuses on expands.

Why do I like this practice of picking one word? Because it tells you a lot about how you think about yourself. Try it. If you could pick only one word to describe yourself, what would it be? I hope it's positive! If it is, it will help you go in the right direction. If it's not, then you need to change your word.

10. Take Responsibility for Your Life

We tend to get in life what we are willing to tolerate. If we allow others to disrespect us, we get disrespected. If we tolerate abuse, we get abused. If we think it's okay to be overworked and underpaid, guess what will happen? The changes you need to make may not be easy, they might not happen quickly. You might have to dig yourself out of a big hole. But you can do it, and it will be worth all the work you put into it.

I wish I could sit down with you, hear your story, and encourage you specifically in your journey. If you've had a difficult time and you don't feel good about yourself, I want to tell you that you do have value. You matter. Your life can change, and you can make a difference—no matter what kind of background you have or where you come from. No matter what traumas you've suffered or mistakes you've made, you can learn and grow. You can become the person you have the potential to be. You just need to believe in yourself to get started. And every time you take a step, think a positive thought, make a good choice, practice a small discipline, you're moving one step closer. Just keep moving forward, and keep believing.

How to Believe in Yourself

1. Make a list of all of your best personal qualities. If you have positive self-esteem, then this will probably be easy for you. If you don't, you may need to spend days or weeks creating the list. Don't stop until you have written a hundred positive things about yourself and then spend time every day reading the list to remind yourself of your value. Using the list as a springboard, decide on the one word that best describes you. Make this word your North Star as you begin adding value to yourself.

2. Few things impact a person's self-esteem more than the way they talk to themselves on a day-to-day basis. Are you aware of how you talk to yourself? Keep track by using your smartphone or carrying an index card so you can tally the number of times each day this week that you think something positive or negative about yourself. In addition, you can ask close friends or family members to tell you whether they think you see yourself in a favorable or unfavorable light.

3. If you aren't doing so already, find a way to serve and add value to others on a weekly basis. Do something that uses your strengths, benefits others, and makes you feel good about yourself. Start small. If you're already serving, then do more. It's a good rule of thumb to give a tenth of your time to serving and adding value to others. So, for example, if you work forty hours a week, devote four hours to serving others.

4

Set Aside Time to Reflect

Learning to Pause Allows Growth to Catch Up with You

There are many different ways of growing and an infinite number of lessons to be learned in life. But there are some kinds of growth that come to us *only* if we are willing to stop, pause, and allow the lesson to catch up with us.

The Power of Pausing

If you're nearly as old as I am, you may remember an old slogan once used by Coca-Cola. They called Coke "the pause that refreshes." That's what reflection is to someone who desires to grow. Learning to pause allows growth to catch up with you.

Here are my observations concerning the power of the pause and how reflection can help you to grow:

1. Reflection Turns Experience into Insight

For over two thousand years, people have been saying that experience is the best teacher. With all due respect, I have to disagree with that statement. Experience is not the best teacher. Evaluated experience is!

There's an old joke that experience is a hard teacher because the test is given first and the lesson is given afterward. That's true, but only if the person takes time to reflect after the experience. Otherwise, you receive the test first and the lesson may never come. People have innumerable experiences every day, and many learn nothing from them because they never take the time to pause and reflect. That's why it is so important to pause and let understanding catch up with us.

2. Pausing Helps You Recognize Life Markers

Stopping to reflect is one of the most valuable activities people can do to grow. It has much greater value to them than even motivation or encouragement because it allows you to make sure you're on the right track. After all, if you are going down the wrong road, you don't need motivation to speed up. You need to stop, reflect, and change course. Most people are pretty busy. There are a lot of demands on them, and they rush from place to place trying to get things done. Along the way, they have certain experiences that are *life markers*. They go to a place or are part of an event or meet a person that in some way marks them for life because something important happened. Often these markers identify for them a time of transition, change, or transformation.

If you don't take the time to pause and reflect, you can miss the significance of such events. Reflection allows those experiences to move from being life *markers* to life *makers*. If you pause to allow growth to catch up with you, it makes your life better, because you can not only better understand the significance of what you've experienced but also implement changes and course corrections as a result. You are also better equipped to teach others from the wisdom you have gained.

3. Pausing with Intention Expands and Enriches Thinking

Study the lives of the great people who have made an impact on the world, and you will find that in virtually every case, they spent a considerable amount of time alone thinking. Every significant religious leader in history spent time in solitude. Every political leader who had an impact on history practiced the discipline of solitude to think and plan. Great artists spend countless hours in their studios or with their instruments not just doing, but exploring their ideas and experiences. Most leading universities give their faculty time not only to teach, but to think, research, and write. Time alone allows people to sort through their experience, put it into perspective, and plan for the future. I strongly encourage you to find a place to think and to discipline yourself to pause and use it, because it has the potential to change your life. It can help you to figure out what's really important and what isn't.

4. When You Take Time to Pause, Use Your I's

When you take the time to pause and reflect, there are really four basic directions your thinking should go:

INVESTIGATION

The great scientist Galileo said, "All truths are easy to understand once they are discovered. The point is to discover them. That takes investigation." Pausing means more than just slowing down to smell the roses. It means stopping and really figuring them out. That generally requires a person to ask questions, which I'll discuss in the next section of this chapter. The thing to remember is that continual growth from experiences is only possible when we discover insights and truths within them. That comes from investigation.

INCUBATION

Incubation is taking an experience of life and putting it into the slow cooker of your mind to simmer for a while. It is very similar to meditation. It's like the "flip side" of prayer. When I pray, I talk to God. When I meditate, I listen to him. Incubation is listening and learning.

ILLUMINATION

Illumination is the discovery of the "aha" moments in your life, the times when you experience sudden realization or insight. It's when the proverbial lightbulb turns on. Few things in life are more rewarding than such moments. I find that I experience moments of illumination only after I spend time investigating an idea and then allowing it to incubate for a period of time. But such moments are the reward for committing time and effort to pausing and reflecting.

ILLUSTRATION

Most good ideas are like skeletons. They provide good structure, but they need meat on their bones. They lack substance, and until they have it, they aren't that useful. What would a party be without sharing good stories? Boring. What about teaching your kids life's important lessons without giving an example they can understand and relate to? Illustrating is the process of putting flesh on ideas.

Good Questions Are the Heart of Reflection

I cannot overemphasize the importance of asking good questions when it comes to personal growth. If your questions are focused, they will stimulate creative thinking. Why? Because there is something about a well-worded question that often penetrates to the heart of the matter and triggers new ideas and insights. If your questions are honest, they will lead to solid convictions. If you ask quality questions, they will help you to create a high-quality life.

Personal Awareness Questions

Here is a series of questions to answer to help you develop personal awareness.

1. What is my biggest asset?
2. What is my biggest liability?
3. What was my highest high?
4. What was my lowest low?
5. What is my most worthwhile emotion?
6. What is my least worthwhile emotion?
7. What is my best habit?
8. What is my worst habit?

9. What is most fulfilling to me?
10. What do I prize most highly?

You can ask yourself questions in just about any area of life to help you pause, focus, and learn. For example, if you wanted to grow in the area of relationships, you could ask yourself the following questions:

1. Do I value people?
2. Do people know I value them?
3. How do I show it?
4. Am I a "plus" or a "minus" in my most important relationships?
5. What evidence do I have to confirm my opinion?
6. What is the love language of the people I love?
7. How can I serve them?
8. Do I need to forgive someone in my life who needs to be given grace?
9. Whom in my life should I take time to thank?
10. Who in my life should be receiving more of my time?

What you want to accomplish in life and where you are in the journey will determine what areas you most need to think about today, tailoring the questions to yourself. But the most important thing you must do is write out the questions and write out the answers. Why? Because you will discover that what you think after you write the answer is different from what you thought before you wrote it. Writing helps you to discover what you truly know, think, and believe.

Worth the Trouble

All of this probably sounds like a lot of steps and a lot of trouble. You're right; it is. That's why most people never do it. But it is worth every bit of effort you put into it. The farther you go in life, the more critical it is that you take time to pause and think. The older you are, the less time you have to stay on purpose and do the things you were created to do. But here's the good news: If you've been diligent in your efforts to grow along the way, you will also be better equipped to fulfill that purpose, even if it requires you to make significant changes or course corrections.

Never forget that your goal in personal growth is embracing and striving to reach your potential. To do that, you need to keep pausing, keep asking questions, and keep growing every day.

How to Set Aside Time to Reflect

1. Have you created a place where you can consistently and effectively pause and reflect? If not, do so immediately. First, figure out what kind of environment will be good for you. Among the places I have chosen over the years are a rock outdoors, a small isolated room where no one would bother me, and a special chair in my office. Figure out what works for you, and stick with it for as long as it's effective.

2. Schedule time to pause and reflect. If you don't, it will always get shuffled off of your to-do list. Ideally, you would spend a short time pausing to reflect at the end of every day (between ten and thirty minutes), a significant time every week (at least an hour or two), part of a day several times a year (half a day), and an extended time annually (as little as a day and as much as a week). Put these times to pause on your calendar and guard them as you would your most important appointments.

3. Where do you most need to grow right now? Is it in self-management? Is there an issue that you can't seem to wrestle down? Are you experiencing a plateau in your career? Are you failing in the most important relationships in your life? Do you need to examine or reexamine your purpose? Do you need

to assess what you should be doing if you are in the second half of your life?

Whatever your issue is, create questions around it and spend time writing your answer to those questions during your scheduled times of reflection.

5

Embrace Discipline Daily

Motivation Gets You Going—Discipline Keeps You Growing

Everyone wants to be encouraged. Everyone enjoys being inspired. But here's the truth when it comes to personal growth: Motivation gets you going, but discipline keeps you growing. It doesn't matter how talented you are. It doesn't matter how many opportunities you receive. If you want to grow, consistency is key.

How to Grow in Consistency

If you want to become more disciplined and consistent in your performance, you need to become more disciplined and consistent in your growth. How can you do that? By knowing the what, how, why, and when of personal improvement. Take some time to consider the following four questions about your growth:

1. Do You Know What You Need to Improve?

All the time I see people with purpose who are inconsistent in their progress. They have the ambition to succeed and they show aptitude for their job, yet they do not move forward. Why? Because they think they can master their job and don't need to master themselves. What a mistake. Your future is dependent on your personal growth. Improving yourself daily guarantees you a future filled with possibilities. The more tuned in you are to your purpose, and the more dedicated you are to growing toward it, the better your chances of reaching your potential, expanding your possibilities, and doing something significant.

2. Do You Know How You Are Supposed to Improve?

Do you have a handle on how to improve yourself? I have four very simple suggestions that can get you started:

MATCH YOUR MOTIVATION TO YOUR PERSONALITY TYPE

Not everyone gets motivated the same way or is motivated by the same things. To give yourself a fighting chance to become consistent in your growth, start by leveraging your personality type to get yourself going. There are dozens of personality profiles and systems that people use. I like the one based on the classic personality types that has been taught by Florence Littauer.

Phlegmatic

Strengths: Easygoing and likable.
Weakness: Inertia.

If you're phlegmatic, motivate yourself by finding the value in what you need to do. When phlegmatics see the value in doing something, they can be one of the most tenacious (meaning stubborn) of all personality types.

Choleric

Strengths: Take charge easily and make decisions quickly.
Weakness: Refuse to participate when not "in charge."

If you are choleric, motivate yourself by focusing on the choices you can make. Every person is in charge of his own growth. Choose how you will grow and stick with it.

Sanguine

Strengths: Fun-loving and often the life of every party.
Weakness: Easily distracted.

If you're sanguine, motivate yourself to grow by making a game of it. If that seems impossible, then give yourself rewards for incremental successes.

Melancholic

Strengths: Perfectionist with great attention to detail.
Weakness: Afraid of making mistakes.

If you are melancholic, motivate yourself by focusing on the joy of learning details and the potential for developing a level of mastery over your subject matter.

As you can see, every personality type has its strengths. You just need to tap that strength in your personality to set yourself up for success when it comes to motivation.

START WITH THE SIMPLE STUFF

When you attempt too much too soon, you're almost guaranteed to fall short of your desired results. That is demotivating. The secret to building motivational momentum is to start small with the simple stuff. Begin by setting goals that are worthwhile but highly achievable. Master the basics. Then practice them every day without fail. Small disciplines repeated with consistency every day lead to great achievements gained slowly over time.

If you want to grow, don't try to win big. Try to win small.

BE PATIENT

If you're an American, as I am, you may agree that as a culture, we have a problem with patience. We want everything fast. We live in a country with fast-food restaurants and fast-weight-loss clinics. How ironic.

When I give the advice to be patient, I am the person who most needs to take it. Impatience is one of my greatest weaknesses. I think it comes from having unrealistic expectations—for myself and others. Everything I want to do takes longer than I anticipate. Every endeavor I lead is more difficult than I believed it would be. Every project I attempt costs more than I expected. Every task I hand off to another person is more complicated than I hoped. Some days I believe that patience is a minor form of despair disguised as a virtue. Maybe you are similar to me.

Most people never realize how close they are to achieving

significant things because they give up too soon. Everything worthwhile in life takes dedication and time. The people who grow and achieve the most are the ones who harness the power of patience and persistence.

VALUE THE PROCESS

One of the best things you can do for yourself as a learner is to cultivate the ability to value and enjoy the process of growth. It is going to take a long time, so you might as well enjoy the journey. You can visualize tomorrow using it as motivation to grow, but if you want to actually grow, your focus needs to be on today. If you value today and find a way to enjoy it, you will invest in today. And the small steps you take today will lead to the bigger steps you take someday.

3. Do You Know Why You Want to Keep Improving?

Knowing *what* to improve and *how* to improve are critical to consistency in personal growth. But so is knowing *why*. The *how* and *what* will take you only so far. The why is what keeps you motivated long after that first rush of energy and enthusiasm wears off. It can carry you through when willpower isn't enough. Think of it as why-power.

Having a strong *why* will help you to keep going when the discipline of learning becomes difficult, discouraging, or tedious. If your growth is connected to your values, dreams, and purpose, you'll know why you're doing it. And you will be more likely to follow through. If you think about it, you can see that discipline and motivation are two sides of the same coin.

If you have the motivation you need, discipline is no problem. If you lack motivation, discipline is always a problem.

When you make the right choices—however small—and do it consistently over time, it can make a huge difference in your life. If you remember *why* you're making those choices, it becomes easier.

4. Do You Know When You Are Supposed to Improve?

The final piece of the puzzle is the question of *when*. When do you need to improve? First the obvious answer: right now. Today. You need to get started if you haven't yet. More important, you need today to be every day.

You will never change your life until you change something you do daily. That means developing great habits. Discipline is the bridge between goals and accomplishments, and that bridge must be crossed every day. Over time that daily crossing becomes a habit. And ultimately, people do not decide their future; they decide their habits and their habits decide their future.

What are you doing daily that needs to change? What needs doing? Maybe more important, what needs undoing? What are you willing to change doing today in order to change what you will be doing tomorrow?

In the end, hard work is really the accumulation of easy things you didn't do when you should have. It's like diet and exercise. Everyone wants to be thin, but no one wants to make the right choices to get there. It's hard work when you've neither eaten right nor exercised day after day. However, if you make small right choices each day, day after day, you see results.

Maybe It's Time to Stop Setting Goals

Consistency isn't easy. You must figure out what works for you, but I'll be glad to tell you what has worked for me. Instead of being goal conscious, I focus on being growth conscious. Here's the difference:

GOAL CONSCIOUSNESS	GROWTH CONSCIOUSNESS
Focuses on a destination	Focuses on the journey
Motivates you and others	Matures you and others
Seasonal	Lifelong
Challenges you	Changes you
Stops when a goal is reached	Keeps you growing beyond the goal

I am such a strong believer in people and in human potential—not only in others but also myself—that I don't ever want to put a lid on it by setting long-term goals that are too small. I did that early in my career, and I realized it would limit me. If you can believe in yourself and the potential that is in you, and then focus on growth instead of goals, there's no telling how far you can grow. You just need to consistently put in the work as you keep believing in yourself. And never forget: Motivation gets you going, but discipline keeps you growing.

How to Embrace Daily Discipline

1. Align your methods of motivation with your personality type. Use whatever personality profile you prefer to study your personality type. (If you haven't used one before, then find one. Examples include Myers-Briggs Type Indicator, DiSC, and Personality Plus.) Once you have a good handle on what makes your personality type tick, then develop a daily growth system that is simple and plays to your strengths.

2. It's difficult to remain engaged in anything if you have not found a way to value and appreciate the process. Make a list of everything you like about personal growth. If your list is very short, really work at it. *Anything* you can find as motivation will help you to develop better growth habits.

3. The more *why*s you have for pursuing personal growth on a daily basis, the more likely you will be to follow through. Start compiling those *why*s. Think of immediate benefits as well as long-term ones. Consider reasons related to purpose, vision, and dreams. Think of how it will help you relationally, vocationally, and spiritually. Any reason to grow is a good reason as long as it's *your* reason.

6

Seek Out a Positive Environment
Growth Thrives in Conducive Surroundings

believe at some point during every person's lifetime, there comes a need to change environments in order to grow. That may seem obvious in the case of someone who grew up in a terrible situation or suffered abuse. But I also believe it's true even for people who grow up in positive, nurturing environments. If we want to grow to reach our potential, we must be in the right environment. That usually requires us to make changes in our life.

Change Depends on Your Choices

You've probably seen the phrase *growth = change*. It's possible to change without growing, but it's impossible to grow without changing. One of the keys to making the right changes that allow us to grow is knowing the difference between a problem or challenge, which you can change, and a fact of life, which you cannot. For example, one day as a teenager I looked into the mirror and came to a sudden realization. I was not a handsome guy. It was a fact of life. I couldn't change my face. What was I going to do? I made a decision. I would change my attitude about it. I would smile. Did it change my face? No, not really. But it helped me to look better.

Like me, you must deal with many facts of life. You cannot change where and when you were born. You cannot change who your parents are. You cannot change your height or your DNA. But you can change your attitude about them. You must do your best to live with them.

A problem is different. A problem is something you *can* do something about. It's something you can *grow* through. How? Ironically, it begins with a similar first step: a change in attitude. When you change your attitude regarding a problem, you open up many opportunities for growth.

When it comes to environment, I believe we need to make the following six choices to put ourselves in a better place for growth:

1. Assess Your Current Environment

Change just for the sake of change is not going to help you. If you are going to make changes, you must make sure they're the right ones. How do you do that? Start by assessing where you are now and why you want to change.

One of the ways to judge whether you're growing and in a conducive growth environment is to discern whether you're looking forward to what you're doing or looking back at what you've done. If the future looks dull, routine, or confining, you may need to start looking to make changes.

You may be able to intuitively sense if you are not in the

kind of environment that is going to promote your growth. However, if you find it difficult to make that judgment about your situation, then you can approach it from another direction. You can ask yourself questions to help you understand who and what nurtures you personally, and then figure out whether or not you're getting those things. Here are the questions I ask: Are others ahead of me? Am I continually challenged? Is my focus forward? Is the atmosphere affirming? Am I often out of my comfort zone? Do I wake up excited? Am I confident despite the prospect of failure? Are others growing? Is change welcomed? Is growth modeled and expected?

The main idea is to know yourself and to assess whether you're getting what you need in your current environment. If you are, celebrate. If you're not, prepare yourself to make some hard choices.

2. Change Yourself and Your Environment

If you know that you need to make a major change to your environment, then there's something you must keep in mind: You must also determine to change yourself at the same time. Here's why: If you try to . . .

Change yourself but not your environment—growth will be slow and difficult;

Change your environment but not yourself—growth will be slow and less difficult;

Change your environment *and* yourself—growth will be faster and more successful.

By putting both together at the same time, you increase and accelerate your chances for success.

As you consider changing yourself and your environment, think about the elements that the right kind of growth environment provide:

The right *soil* to grow in: What nourishes me? Growth.
The right *air* to breathe in: What keeps me alive? Purpose.
The right *climate* to live in: What sustains me? People.

They say that if you put a pumpkin in a jug when it's the size of a walnut, it will grow to the size and shape of the jug and never get bigger. That can happen to a person's thinking. Don't allow that to happen to you.

3. Change Whom You Spend Your Time With

According to research by social psychologist Dr. David McClelland of Harvard, the people with whom you habitually associate are called your "reference group," and these people determine as much as 95 percent of your success or failure in life.

It is not always comfortable, but it is always profitable to associate with people larger than ourselves. People with integrity. People who are positive. People who are ahead of us professionally. People who lift us up instead of knocking us down. People who take the high road, never the low. And above all, people who are growing.

I highly recommend that you also find an accountability partner to take the growth journey with you. That person will help you to stick with your right decisions and help you avoid making wrong ones. A good accountability partner should:

> Love you unconditionally.
> Desire your success.
> Be mature.
> Ask you agreed-on questions.
> Help you when you need help.

You cannot take the growth journey alone, not if you want to reach your potential. The most significant factor in any person's environment is the people. If you change nothing else in your life for the better than that, you will have increased your chances of success tenfold. So think long and hard about whom you're spending the most time with, for wherever they are headed, so are you.

4. Challenge Yourself in Your New Environment

One of the most positive things about being in a growth environment is that it gives you room to embrace and expand your potential, but you must be intentional about finding and creating those growth opportunities. You must develop the habit and discipline of challenging yourself.

One way to challenge yourself is by making your goals public. Few things push a person like a deadline and an audience. That doesn't mean that you will always reach your goals. But you will likely find that if you tell others about what you intend to do, you will work harder and in such a way that you won't be ashamed of your efforts even if everyone is watching them.

Another way to challenge yourself is to look for one major growth opportunity every week, follow through on it, and learn from it. Whether it's meeting with friends, scheduling a learning lunch with a mentor, or attending a conference or event in the area you want to grow in, always prepare by asking these five questions before the learning time:

- **What are their strengths?** This is where you'll learn the most.
- **What are they learning now?** This is how you can catch their passion.
- **What do I need right now?** This helps you to apply what you learn to your situation.
- **Whom have they met, what have they read, or what have they done that has helped them?** This helps you to find additional growth opportunities.
- **What haven't I asked that I should have?** This enables them to point out changes you need to make from their perspective.

A better growth environment won't help you much if you don't do everything in your power to make the most of it. You must seize the growth opportunities you have and make the most of them by challenging yourself.

5. Focus on the Moment

The changes we want to make in our lives come only in the present. What we do *now* controls who we become and where we are in the future. We live and work in the present. If you need to make changes in yourself and your environment, don't worry about your past. Mother Teresa observed, "Yesterday is gone. Tomorrow has not yet come. We have only today. Let us begin." If you need to make changes in yourself and your environment, don't dwell on your past. You can't change it. Don't worry about your future. You can't control it. Focus on the current moment and what you can do now.

6. Move Forward Despite Criticism

Growth always comes from taking action, and taking action almost always brings criticism. Move forward anyway. To reach your potential, you must do not only what others believe you cannot do, but what even *you* believe you cannot do. Most people underestimate themselves. They shoot for what they know they can reach. Instead they should reach for what's beyond their grasp. If you don't try to create the future you want, you must endure the future you get.

As you take action to change yourself and your environment, you will almost certainly be criticized for it. Poet Ralph Waldo Emerson observed, "Whatever course you decide upon, there is always someone to tell you that you are wrong. There are always difficulties arising which tempt you to believe that your critics are right. To map out a plan of action and follow it to the end requires some of the same courage which a soldier needs. Peace has its victories, but it takes brave men to win them." Before making a major change, seek wise counsel if you can, but make your own decisions. You are ultimately accountable for the choices you make in your life.

How to Seek Out a Positive Environment

1. Assess your current environment when it comes to growth by answering true or false to each of the following ten statements:

1. Others are ahead of me learning.
2. I am continually challenged.
3. My focus is forward.
4. The atmosphere is affirming.
5. I am often out of my comfort zone.
6. I wake up excited.
7. Failure is not my enemy.
8. Others are growing.
9. People desire change.
10. Growth is modeled and expected.

If you answer false to more than five of the statements, your current environment may be hampering your growth. You will need to determine whether you need to change or improve your environment in order to reach your potential.

2. Assess your personal-growth needs in the three main areas mentioned in the chapter:

THE RIGHT SOIL TO GROW IN:
WHAT NOURISHES ME? GROWTH.

Use the following list to assess what nurtures you:

Music—What songs lift me?
Thoughts—What ideas speak to me?
Experiences—What experiences rejuvenate me?
Friends—What people encourage me?
Recreation—What activities revive me?
Soul—What spiritual exercises strengthen me?
Hopes—What dreams inspire me?
Home—What family members care for me?
Giftedness—What blessings activate me?
Memories—What recollections make me smile?
Books—What have I read that changed me?

THE RIGHT AIR TO BREATHE IN:
WHAT KEEPS ME ALIVE? PURPOSE.

Review your answers to the questions at the end of chapter 3 and chapter 5. Use them to develop a purpose statement for your life. Don't expect it to be perfect or permanent. It will probably continue to grow and change as you do, but it will give you a stronger sense of direction now.

THE RIGHT CLIMATE TO LIVE IN:
WHAT SUSTAINS ME? PEOPLE.

Make a list of the people who are currently most influential in your life: friends, family, colleagues, employers, mentors, and so on. Be sure to also include anyone you spend a substantial amount of time with. Then scan the list and determine who on the list is "larger" than you: more skilled or more talented, farther ahead professionally, more solid in character or in any other significant way. If the majority of people are not stretching you, you need to find additional people who will help you change and grow.

3. Significant growth will not occur in your life if you are not continually challenged in your environment. Set specific goals for yourself that are beyond your current capabilities. In addition, review your calendar for the upcoming month. Look for the best potential growth opportunity in each week and plan for it by asking yourself questions similar to the ones contained in this chapter.

7

Become Highly Strategic

To Maximize Growth, Develop Strategies

Most people allow their lives to simply happen to them. They float along. They wait. They react. And by the time a large portion of their life is behind them, they realize they should have been more proactive and strategic. I hope that hasn't been true for you. If it has, then I want to encourage you to develop a stronger sense of urgency and a pro-strategic mind-set. As you plan and develop strategies for your life and growth, I want to share with you some of the things I've learned that have helped me in the process.

1. Life Is Very Simple, but Keeping It That Way Is Very Difficult

Despite what others might say, I believe life is pretty simple. It's a matter of knowing your values, making some key decisions based on those values, and then managing those decisions on a day-to-day basis. That's pretty straightforward. And at least in theory, the longer we live and the more we learn, the more experience and the more knowledge we acquire that should make life even simpler. But life has a way of *becoming* complicated, and it is only through great effort that we can keep it simple. A beautifully conceived strategy does you no good if you can't use it.

2. Designing Your Life Is More Important Than Designing Your Career

If you plan your life well, then your career will work itself out. The problem is that most people don't spend very much time planning their careers either. They spend more time planning for Christmas or their vacation. Why? Because people focus on what they think will give them the greatest return. If you don't believe you can succeed in your life in the long term, you're not very likely to give it the planning attention it deserves.

Planning your life is about finding yourself, knowing who you are, and then customizing a design for your growth. Once you draw the blueprint for your life, then you can apply it to your career.

3. Life Is Not a Dress Rehearsal!

There is no warm-up for life, no dress rehearsal, yet that's the way many people seem to be treating it. Each of us goes on stage cold, with no preparation, and we have to figure it out as we go along. That can be messy. We fail. We make mistakes. But we still need to give it our best from the very start.

Regret over not being proactive enough is a common theme among people looking back on their lives. We don't get a rehearsal for life. We have to do the best we can in the moment. But we can learn from others who have gone before us. They should inspire us to plan as best we can and then give our all.

4. In Planning Your Life, Multiply Everything by Two

The important things in life usually take longer than we expect and cost more than we anticipate. That is especially true when it comes to personal growth. So what do you do to compensate? Multiply by two. If you think something will take you an hour to do, plan for double to stay out of trouble. If you think a project will take a week to accomplish, allot two. If you think a goal will require $1,000 to fund, set aside $2,000. Two isn't a magic number—it just seems to work for me. I've found that multiplying everything by two infuses realism into my optimism.

I think all people naturally desire for things to come to them quickly and easily, including personal growth. The secret isn't really to want more or want it faster. It's to put more time and attention into what you have and what you can do now. Give three times the effort and energy to growing yourself. And allow yourself to grow slowly and with deep roots. Remember that a squash vine or tomato plant grows in a matter of weeks, produces for several days or weeks, and then dies when the first frost comes. In comparison, a tree grows slowly—over years, decades, or even centuries; it produces fruit for decades; and if healthy, it stands up to frost, storms, and drought.

As you develop strategies for growth, give yourself the time and resources you need. Whatever amounts seem reasonable to you, multiply them by two. That practice will help to keep you from becoming discouraged and giving up too soon.

To Develop Strategies, Depend on Systems

Most accomplishments in life come more easily if you approach them strategically. Rarely does a haphazard approach to anything succeed. And even the few times a nonstrategic approach to achievement comes to fruition, it's not repeatable. So how do you accomplish something strategically on a consistent basis? By creating and using systems.

What is a system? It's a process for predictably achieving a goal based on specific, orderly, repeatable principles and practices. Systems leverage your time, money, and abilities. They are great tools for personal growth. Systems are deliberate, intentional, and practical. They really work—regardless of your profession, talent level, or experience. They improve your performance. A life without any systems is a life where the person must face every task and challenge from scratch.

If you want to make the most of your personal growth by getting the most you can out of every effort and doing it as efficiently as possible, you need to develop systems that work for you. That will be a personal thing, because your systems need to be tailored to you. However, as you strive to create them, keep the following guidelines in mind:

1. Effective Systems Take the Big Picture into Account

People who excel, regardless of their profession, develop systems to help them achieve the big picture. It's not enough to be busy. If you're busy planning, busy reading books, and busy going to conferences, but these activities aren't targeted on the areas essential to your success, you're not helping yourself. As the saying goes, unhappiness is not knowing what we want and killing ourselves to get it.

What is your big picture? In what areas must you grow to achieve your purpose? And what systems can you develop to advance yourself in those areas today and every day? I had to stop reading books simply for pleasure and read books that would help me in my areas of strength. I also took two speed-reading classes to help me improve. What must you do?

2. Effective Systems Make Use of Priorities

A system is of limited help to you if it doesn't take into account your priorities. Brian Tracy says, "Perhaps the very best question you can memorize and repeat over and over is, 'What is the most valuable use of my time right now?'" Your answer to that question should shape any system you create for yourself. You should also ask yourself, "*When* is my most valuable time?" because you'll want to always make the most of it.

What systems do you need to put into place to help you maintain your priorities? And what people do you need to give responsibility and power to so they can help you?

3. Effective Systems Include Measurement

Any kind of progress requires the ability to measure, and for that reason, your systems must include a way to measure your results. Think about it: Where would businesspeople be if they had no way of measuring their profits? Where would sales and marketing people be if they had no idea how many leads turned into sales or how many people responded to advertising? Where would sports teams be if they never knew the score of the game? Measurement is key to improvement. In fact, measurement itself can even create improvement. Researchers who conducted experiments in productivity at the Hawthorne Works Plant outside Chicago in the 1930s discovered that when people knew their work was being measured, their productivity increased. Researchers called that the Hawthorne Effect.

Measurement enables you to set goals, evaluate progress, judge results, and diagnose problems. If you want to stimulate your growth progress and evaluate the results, build measurement into your systems.

4. Effective Systems Include Application

It's not enough just to plan, though planning is important. Both plan and action must go together. The plan creates the track. The action provides the traction. So anytime you have a goal but you think you won't be able to reach it, don't adjust the goal. Adjust the action steps.

People who develop systems that include action steps are almost always more successful than people who don't. Even less talented people with fewer resources accomplish more if they have developed the habit of taking action. That's one of the reasons I've developed the habit of asking myself three questions every time I learn something new:

- Where can I use this?
- When can I use this?
- Who needs to know this?

This has become a discipline in my life, so I always have a bias toward action when I learn something new.

5. Effective Systems Employ Organization

Time has a way of getting away from most people, yet time is what life is made of. Everything we do requires time, yet many people take it for granted. How you spend your time is more important than how you spend your money. Money mistakes can be corrected. But once time has passed, it's gone forever.

Being organized gives a sense of power. When you know your purpose and priorities and you have ordered your day, week, or year according to them, you have a clarity of thought that strengthens everything you do. You develop an efficiency that helps you to follow through on everything you do. There are few things like it. Make sure your systems make you as organized as you can possibly be.

6. Effective Systems Promote Consistency

If you want to succeed in the long run, you must learn to be consistent day in and day out, week in and week out, year in and year out. You will never change your life until you change something you do daily. The secret of your success is found in your daily routine. So any system you develop needs to promote consistency, and you must follow it consistently.

What does it take to develop consistency? A system and the discipline to follow through. Most efforts at consistency are not so exciting. Every now and then, I get requests from people who say they want to spend the day with me. I think they would be very disappointed by how boring my average day is. I'm up early and spend hours at my desk. In the afternoon I exercise and take care of people-related responsibilities. And I usually go to bed by 10:00. It's not exciting, but it is consistent. And it's a system that works for me.

As you seek to develop strategies to maximize your growth, you should also seek out principles that have stood the test of time. Don't try to simply adopt someone else's practices as your own. Customize them to yourself. Use them to build your strengths and reach your goals. And remember that, as Jim Rohn said, "If you go to work on your goals, your goals will go to work on you. If you go to work on your plan, your plan will go to work on you. Whatever good things we build end up building us." That's why you need to become highly strategic.

How to Become Highly Strategic

1. Take some time to assess which areas in your life receive the most of your strategic planning time. Here is a list of areas to get you thinking. Add others that apply to you:

> Career
> Faith
> Family
> Health
> Hobby
> Marriage
> Personal Growth
> Vacation

Have you been strategic in your approach to designing strategies and systems for your life? If not, why not? If so, where have you placed the most emphasis? Does your past behavior line up with what you *say* your priorities are? How would you like them to be?

2. Begin developing (or refining) systems for yourself that will maximize your time and increase your efficiency. Brainstorm a list of areas where you desire to improve, are experiencing a problem, or sensing an opportunity. Try to create a system to help you for each. As you design them, make sure that each takes into account the following:

The Big Picture—Will the system help you reach your big-picture goals?

Your Priorities—Is the system consistent with your values and commitments?

Measurement—Does the system give you a tangible way to judge whether you've succeeded?

Application—Does the system have a built-in bias toward action?

Organization—Does the system make better use of your time than what you're doing now?

Consistency—Can and will you easily repeat the system on a regular basis?

Don't be reluctant to make adjustments to systems you develop or even to abandon them if they don't serve you well. However, you may want to try out any system you develop for at least three weeks (the normal time needed to start developing a positive habit) before evaluating its validity.

3. Many people who try to develop strategies for their life and growth make them too complicated. Any system you develop should be simple and straightforward. To test the ones you develop, try this: Explain them to a friend to see if they pass two tests. The first is whether you can explain it clearly. If you can't, it may be too complicated. The second is to see if your friend knows of a better or simpler way of achieving the same goal.

8

Turn Negatives into Positives

Good Management of Bad Experiences Leads to Great Growth

How do you usually respond to bad experiences? Do you explode in anger? Do you shrink into yourself emotionally? Do you detach yourself from the experience as much as possible? Do you ignore it?

Each time we encounter a painful experience, we get to know ourselves a little better. Pain can stop us dead in our tracks. Or it can cause us to make decisions we would like to put off, deal with issues we would rather not face, and make changes that make us feel uncomfortable. Pain prompts us to face who we are and where we are. What we do with that experience defines who we become.

What I Know about Bad Experiences

What separates people who thrive from those who merely survive? I believe it's how they face their problems. I've never known anyone who said, "I love problems," but I've known many who have admitted that their greatest gains came in the middle of their pain.

Here's what I know about bad experiences:

1. Everyone Has Them

Life is filled with ups and downs. The problem is that what most of us want is ups and ups. That's not possible. I think it's pretty obvious that nobody gets to escape bad experiences. Perhaps that's one of the reasons my speech "How to Do Good When Things Are So Bad" has been so popular. As the saying goes: Some days you're the pigeon; some days you're the statue!

We can do everything in our power to avoid negative experiences, but they have a way of finding us. No matter who you are, where you live, what you do, or what your background is, you will have to deal with bad experiences. You have to have realistic expectations when it comes to pain and problems. You can't avoid them.

2. No One Likes Them

You don't like it when you're in the middle of a bad experience. Neither do I. No one expects us to like such things. They're just painful. But if we can manage the experience well, then we can actually find a way to enjoy talking about it afterward. It can become a great war story.

3. Few People Make Bad Experiences Positive Experiences

Life's difficulties do not allow us to stay the same. They move us. The question is, in which direction will we be moved:

forward or backward? When we have bad experiences, do we become better or bitter? Will those experiences limit us or lead us to grow?

When tough times come, many people don't respond well. That is why learning to turn negatives into positives is essential for individuals who want to grow and reach their potential. Most successful people will point to the hard times in their lives as key points in their journey of development. If you are dedicated to growth, then you must become committed to managing your bad experiences well.

My Pain File

Everyone has a pain file. You've got yours; I've got mine. Here are a few negative experiences that have become positive gains in growth for me over the long run:

- **The Pain of Inexperience**—I expected instant success early in my career but stumbled often because of my immaturity. I had to learn patience and earn respect and influence from others.
- **The Pain of Incompetence**—I did a lot of counseling early in my career and was terrible at it. That forced me to reevaluate my gifting. Only when I started equipping people did I find my strength zone.
- **The Pain of Disappointment**—Margaret and I were scheduled to adopt a son but then "lost" him. We were devastated. Six months later we adopted our son, Joel, who is a great joy in our lives.
- **The Pain of Conflict**—One church I led experienced

a split in the congregation, and some people left the church. That experience made me dig deeper as a leader.

- **The Pain of Change**—Early in my career I changed organizations. That meant I had to start over. Though difficult, it afforded me many opportunities.
- **The Pain of Bad Health**—My heart attack at age fifty-one was excruciating. It was also an eye-opener. I immediately changed my eating habits and bought into the practice of daily exercise.
- **The Pain of Hard Decisions**—Wanting everyone to be happy and making tough decisions were incompatible tasks. I learned that good leadership is disappointing people at a rate they can stand.
- **The Pain of Financial Loss**—A bad investment decision cost us greatly. It wasn't fun selling my assets to cover it. It helped me to be more careful in risk taking.
- **The Pain of Relationship Losses**—Striving to reach my potential has separated me from friends who had no desire to grow. As I developed new friendships, I learned to build relationships with growing people who wanted to take the journey with me.
- **The Pain of Not Being Number One**—In one job I followed a wonderful founding pastor who was greatly loved as a leader. I was never as loved or respected by some people as much he was. That taught me humility.
- **The Pain of Traveling**—My career has kept me on the road. It taught me to value my family and motivated me to make the most of our time together.

- **The Pain of Responsibility**—Leading organizations and having many people depend on me has required me to think of others' well-being, continually create new content, keep my calendar full, and constantly meet demanding deadlines. This has been very tiring. But it also has taught me a lot about priorities and self-discipline.

What have all these painful experiences taught me? To let my discomfort be a catalyst for my development. Growth is the best possible outcome for any negative experience.

How to Turn Your Pain into Gain

If you want your bad experiences to keep you not only from doing the same silly things but to also lead to significant growth, I suggest that you embrace the following five actions:

1. Choose a Positive Life Stance

"Life stance" is a term used to describe people's overall frame of reference—the set of attitudes, assumptions, and expectations people hold about themselves, other people, and the world in general. It comprises, for instance, people's attitudes toward money, assumptions about their health, and expectations for their children's future. The product of any person's life stance is their overall way of looking at things: whether they tend to be optimistic or pessimistic, cheerful or gloomy, trusting or suspicious, friendly or reserved, brave or timid, generous or stingy, giving or selfish. If you can maintain a positive life stance, you put yourself in the best position to manage bad experiences and turn them into positive growth.

Family therapy pioneer and author Virginia Satir observed, "Life is not the way it's supposed to be. It's the way it is. The way you cope with it is what makes the difference." You cannot control much of what happens to you in life. However, you can control your attitude. And you can choose to rise above your circumstances and refuse to allow negative experiences to undermine who you are and what you believe.

I have come to adopt a positive life stance because I believe it gives me the best chance to succeed while putting me in the best position to help others succeed. To a large degree in life, you get what you expect—not always, but most of the time. So why would I want to expect the worst?

2. Embrace and Develop Your Creativity

The people who make the most of bad experiences are the ones who find creative ways to meet them. They see possibilities within their problems. I believe that creativity begins at the end of your comfort zone. When you feel the pain of bad experiences, creativity gives you the opportunity to turn that pain into gain. The secret to doing that is to use the energy that comes from either adrenaline or anger and use it to solve problems and learn lessons.

When you have a bad experience, instead of letting it discourage you or make you angry, try to find a way to let it prompt your creativity.

3. Embrace the Value of Bad Experiences

It's always easier to see something positive in a negative experience *long after* it happens. It's difficult to meet the negative experience in the moment with a positive mind-set. However, if you can do that, you will always be able to learn something from it.

Where there is no struggle, there is no progress. Facing difficulties is inevitable. Learning from them is optional. Whether you learn is based on if you understand that difficulties present opportunities to learn and treat them accordingly.

4. Make Good Changes After Learning from Bad Experiences

The ability to turn negatives into positives gives us an opportunity to turn our lives around. A bend in the road is not the end of the road unless you fail to make the turn.

Most people don't think their way to positive change—they feel their way. When bad experiences create strong feelings in us, we either face the feelings and try to change or we try to escape. It's the old fight-or-flight instinct. We need to train ourselves to fight for positive changes. How do we do that? By remembering that our choices will lead to either the pain of self-discipline or the pain of regret. I'd rather live with the pain of self-discipline and reap the positive rewards than live with the pain of regret, which can create a deep and continual ache within us.

The next time you find yourself in the midst of a bad experience, remind yourself that you are on the cusp of an opportunity to change and grow. Whether you do will depend on how you react to your experience, and the changes you make as a result. Allow your emotions to be the catalyst for change, think through how to change to make sure you are making good choices, and then take action.

5. Take Responsibility for Your Life

Earlier I said that you need to recognize that your circumstances don't define you. They are outside of you and need not negatively impact your values and standards. At the same time, you must take responsibility for your life and the choices you make.

It is nearly impossible to grow in any significant way when you don't take responsibility for yourself and your life.

No matter what you have gone through in your life—or what you are currently going through—you have the opportunity to grow from it. It's sometimes very difficult to see the opportunity in the midst of the pain, but it is there. You must be willing to not only look for it, but pursue it.

How to Turn Negatives into Positives

1. Assess your attitude toward negative experiences up to this point in your life. Based on your personal history, which of the following statements best describes how you have approached failure, tragedy, problems, and challenges that have caused you pain?

- I do anything and everything possible to avoid pain at all costs.
- I know pain is inevitable, but I try to ignore it or block it out.
- I know everyone experiences pain, so I just endure it when it comes.
- I don't like pain, but I try to remain positive despite it.
- I process the emotion of painful experiences quickly and try to find a lesson in them.
- I process pain, find the lesson, and make changes proactively as a result.

Your goal should be to progress from wherever you are currently on the above scale to the place where you make positive changes in the wake of bad experiences.

2. In the past have you used bad experiences as a springboard for using your creativity? If not, use a current difficulty to help you learn how to become more creative by doing the following:

Define the problem.
Understand your emotion.
Articulate the lesson.
Identify a desired change.
Brainstorm numerous pathways.
Receive others' input.
Implement a course of action.

Remember, if you always do what you've always done, you'll always get what you've always gotten. If you want to arrive at a new destination, you need to take a new path.

3. No insight, no matter how profound, has value to you unless it is attached to changes that you will make based on what you've learned. Personal development requires a bias toward action!

Spend some time recalling the last five bad experiences you've had in your life. Write down each experience, along with what—if anything—you learned from it. Then evaluate whether you decided to make changes based on what you learned and rate yourself on how well you did at implementing those changes in your life. Once you've assessed each bad experience, give yourself a grade from A to F on how well you managed those experiences. If you haven't been an A or B student, you need to use the steps listed above to become better at the process.

9

Grow from the Inside Out

Character Growth Determines the Height of Your Personal Growth

It comes as little surprise that people want to work with people of good character. No one likes to work with unreliable people. But before you or I work with any other person or follow any other leader, whom do we have to rely on every day? Ourselves! That's why character is so important. If you cannot trust yourself, you won't ever be able to grow. Character growth determines the height of your personal growth. And without personal growth, you can never reach your potential. Good character, with honesty and integrity at its core, is essential to success in any area of life. Without it, a person is building on shifting sand.

Most people focus too much on competence and too little on character. How often does a person miss a deadline because he didn't follow through when he should have? How many times do people get lower grades on tests than they could have because they didn't study as much as they should have? How frequently do people fail to grow not because they didn't have time to read helpful books but because they chose to spend their time and money on something else that was less worthwhile? All of those shortcomings are the result of character, not capacity. Character growth determines the height of your personal growth. That's why you need to grow from the inside out.

Rungs on My Character Ladder

Climbing the ladder of character is something that I have always had to do intentionally. It doesn't just happen for me. It probably doesn't just happen for you either. It's taken me decades to develop the right mind-set and learn what "rungs" need to be in place in order for me to improve. Here are the ones on my character ladder that have empowered me to climb higher. Perhaps they will also help you to climb.

1. I Will Focus on Being Better on the Inside than on the Outside—Character Matters

I believe it is a normal human desire to be concerned about how we look on the outside. There's nothing wrong with that. What can get us in trouble is worrying more about how we look on the outside than about how we really are on the inside. Our reputation comes from what others believe about our outside. Our character represents who we are on the inside. And the good news is that if you focus on being better on the inside than on the outside, over time you will also become better on the outside. Why do I say that?

The Inside Influences the Outside

What we believe really matters. We reap what we sow. What we do or neglect to do in the privacy of our daily lives impacts who we are. If you neglect your heart, mind, and soul, it changes who you are on the outside as well as on the inside.

Inside Victories Precede Outside Ones

If you do the things you need to do when you need to do them, then someday you can do the things you want to do when you want to do them. In other words, before you can *do*, you must *be*.

I have often observed people who seemed to be doing all the right things on the outside, yet they were not experiencing success. When that happens, I usually conclude that something is wrong on the inside and needs to be changed. The right motions outwardly with wrong motives inwardly will not bring lasting progress. Right outward talking with wrong inward thinking will not bring lasting success. Expressions of care on the outside with a heart of hatred or contempt on the inside will not bring lasting peace. Continual growth and lasting success are the result of aligning the inside and the outside of our lives. And getting the inside right must come first—with solid character traits that provide the foundation for growth.

Our Inside Development Is Totally Within Our Control

We often cannot determine what happens to us, but we can always determine what happens within us. When we fail to make the right character choices within us, we give away ownership of ourselves. We belong to others—to whatever gains control of us. And that puts us in a bad place. How can you ever reach your potential and become the person you can be if others are making your choices for you?

The "rungs" on my character ladder have come as the result of hard-fought personal choices. They were not easily made and they are not easily managed. Every day there is a battle from the outside for me to compromise or surrender them. Regretfully, there have been times when I have. But whenever that's happened, I have diligently gone after them to return them to their respectful place...inside of me.

2. I Will Follow the Golden Rule—People Matter

Following the golden rule—"Do unto others as you would have them do unto you."—is a wonderful character builder. It prompts you to focus on other people. It leads you to be empathetic. It encourages you to take the high road. And if you stick to it—especially when it's difficult—you can't help but become the kind of person others want to be around. After all, in the end in all of our relationships we are either plusses or minuses in the lives of others. The golden rule helps us to remain a plus.

3. I Will Teach Only What I Believe—Passion Matters

When I was first starting out in my career, there were a few things I taught that I didn't buy into a hundred percent. I'm not talking about things that are clearly right or wrong. I'm talking about subjective things that are a matter of opinion. But as soon as I spoke about them, I regretted it. Do you know what they call a speaker who teaches what he doesn't believe? A hypocrite! So early on, I vowed to teach only what I believe. And that has benefited me, not only in the area of integrity, but also in the area of passion. Borrowed beliefs have no passion, therefore no power. Some of the things I was passionate about thirty years ago, I'm still just as passionate about today.

Individuals who lack principles and passion become bland, colorless people. I don't ever want to become one of those. I bet you don't want to either.

4. I Will Value Humility Above All Virtues—Perspective Matters

I think anyone who is honest with himself realizes that he falls short of where he could and should be in life. Contrary to what Tom Hanks says as Forrest Gump, life is not a box of chocolates. It's more like a jar of jalapeños. What we do today might burn our butts tomorrow!

We don't intend to make mistakes and to fall short, but we do. We're all just one step away from stupid. So how do we keep from taking that step?

REMEMBER THE BIG PICTURE

I think the first thing to do is remind ourselves of the big picture. It's said that President John F. Kennedy kept a small plaque in the White House with the inscription "Oh God, thy sea is so great and my boat is so small." If the person known as the leader of the free world can keep perspective of his true place in the world, so should we.

RECOGNIZE THAT EVERYONE HAS WEAKNESSES

Rick Warren gives good advice about how to remain humble. He suggests admitting our weaknesses, being patient with others' weaknesses, and being open to correction. Of those three things, I have to admit that I do only one of them fairly well. I don't find it difficult to admit my weaknesses—maybe because I have so many. I have a much harder time being patient with others. I am constantly having to remind myself to extend grace to others. And in order to be more open to correction, I never assume that I will not mess up, I develop relationships with good people who will speak the truth to me, and I set up accountability systems in my life.

BE TEACHABLE

I love being around people who have a beginner's mind-set. They think of themselves as apprentices instead of experts and, as a result, have a humble, teachable posture. They try to see things from others' perspective. They are open to new ideas. They possess a thirst for knowledge. They ask questions and know how to listen. And they gather as much information as possible before making decisions. I admire such people and try to be like them.

BE WILLING TO SERVE OTHERS

Few things are better for cultivating character and developing humility than serving others. Putting others first right-sizes our egos and perspective. How does a person who is used to winning remind himself that it's not all about him? By serving others. For me, service starts with Margaret and the rest of my family. Also, beginning in 1997, I've selected a handful of individuals every year whom I can try to serve without receiving anything in return. And I also look for ways to serve my team, since they work so hard to serve me and our vision every day.

BE GRATEFUL

Everything we do, every accomplishment we have, every milestone we pass has come in part because of the efforts of others. There are no self-made men or women. If we can remember that, we can be grateful. And if we are grateful, we are more likely to develop good character than if we aren't.

Confucius asserted, "Humility is the solid foundation of all the virtues." In other words, it paves the way for character growth. And that sets us up for personal growth. These things are definitely connected.

5. I Will Strive to Finish Well—Faithfulness Matters

The final "rung" on my character ladder is the determination to keep building character and living at the highest standard until the day I die. I am endeavoring to do that by doing the right thing and becoming a better person every day. To do the right thing, I don't wait to feel like it. I recognize that emotion follows motion. Do the right thing and you feel right. Do the wrong thing and you feel bad. If you take control of your behavior, your emotions will fall into place. If we focus on personal character, we make the world a better place. If we do that our entire lives, we've done the best thing we can do to improve our world.

The Stronger Your Character, the Greater Your Growth Potential

If we desire to grow and reach our potential, we must pay more attention to our character than to our success. We must recognize that personal growth means more than expanding our minds and adding to our skills. It means increasing our capacity as human beings. It means maintaining core integrity, even when it hurts. It means being who we should be, not just being where we want to be. It means maturing our souls.

Physician and author Orison Swett Marden once described a successful person by saying, "He was born mud and died marble. This gives us an interesting metaphor to use to look at various lives. Some people are born mud and remain mud...Sadly, some are born marble and die mud; some are born mud, dream of marble, but remain mud. But many persons of high character have been born mud and died marble."

Isn't that a wonderful thought? I hope that can be said of me at the end of my life, and I hope the same for you.

How to Grow from the Inside Out

1. Assess where you have put most of your focus up until this point in your life. Has it been on improving on the inside or on the outside? Here are some of the ways you can do that: Compare how much you spent in the last twelve months on clothing, jewelry, accessories, and so on, versus how much you spent on books, conferences, and that sort of thing. Compare how much time you spent in the last month on personal and spiritual growth versus activities related to appearance. If you exercise regularly, examine what benefits you are striving for: Do they relate to inner health or outer appearance?

If your assessment reveals more of an outward focus than an inward one, then determine how to shift your focus by adding time, money, and attention to the things that will make you grow even if they do not show.

2. Plan to spend time in the coming months to regularly serve others. Putting aside your own agenda and putting others first will help you to develop humility, character, and others-mindedness. Start with your family if you aren't in the habit of doing things for them.

Another idea is to set aside at least an hour every week for volunteering. Schedule it, and then give it a hundred percent of your focus while you're serving.

3. What are you doing every day to develop the habit of character growth? Are you giving attention to your soul? Are you doing hard or unpleasant things? Are you practicing the golden rule and putting others ahead of yourself? Your character isn't set. You can improve it. It's never too late. You can change who you are and your overall potential by becoming a better person.

10

Get Used to Stretching Yourself

Growth Stops When You Lose the Tension Between Where You Are and Where You Could Be

As I prepared to write this chapter, I was reminded of all the professional stretching I've had to do over the course of my career. One of my favorite quotes, which I collected as a teenager says, "God's gift to us: potential. Our gift to God: developing it."

Many years ago, during one of the sessions I taught at a leadership conference, I put a rubber band on the table at the place of every attendee. Then I started the session by asking about all the ways people could think of for using them. At the end of the discussion time, I asked them if they could identify the one thing all of their uses had in common. Maybe you've already guessed what it was. Rubber bands are useful only when they are stretched!

That can also be said of us. We have the greatest value when we are stretched. And only by continually stretching—

not only physically but also mentally, emotionally, and spiritually—will we reach our potential.

Here is why stretching has such great value:

1. Few People Want to Stretch

Most people use only a small fraction of their ability and rarely strive to reach their full potential. There is no tension to grow in their lives, little desire to stretch. Too many people are willing to settle for average in life.

I cannot stand the idea of settling for average, can you? Nobody admires average. The best organizations don't pay for average. Mediocrity is not worth shooting for. We must be aware of the gap that stands between us and our potential, and let the tension of that gap motivate us to keep striving to become better.

2. Settling for the Status Quo Ultimately Leads to Dissatisfaction

I believe most people are naturally tempted to settle into a comfort zone where they choose comfort over potential. They fall into familiar patterns and habits, doing the same things in the same ways with the same people at the same time and getting the same results. It's true that being in your comfort zone may feel good, but it leads to mediocrity and, therefore, dissatisfaction.

If you have ever settled for the status quo and then wondered why your life isn't going the way you'd hoped, then you need to realize that you will only reach your potential if you have the courage to push yourself outside your comfort zone and break out of a mind-set of mediocrity. You must be willing to leave behind what feels familiar, safe, and secure. You must give up excuses and push forward. You must be willing to face the tension that comes from stretching toward your potential.

3. Stretching Always Starts from the Inside Out

Most people have a dream. For some, it's on the tip of their tongue, and for others, it's buried deep in their hearts, but everyone has one. However, not very many people are pursuing it. What is stopping them? For that matter, what is stopping you? Most Americans want to lose weight, but they don't make the effort to do so. I run across people all the time who tell me that they want to write a book, but when I ask, "Have you started writing?" the answer is almost always no. Instead of wishing, wanting, and waiting, people need to search inside themselves for reasons to start.

It's wise to remember that our situation in life is mainly due to the choices we make and the actions we take—or fail to take. The older we are, the more responsible we are for our situation. If you are merely average or if you are no closer to your dream this year than you were last year, you can choose to accept it, defend it, cover it up, and explain it away. Or you can choose to change it, grow from it, and forge a new path.

Where do you find the internal impetus for stretching? Measure what you're doing against what you're capable of. Measure yourself against yourself. Make a contest of it. If you have no idea what you might be capable of, talk to people who care about you and believe in you. Don't have any people in your life who fit that description? Then go look for some. Find a mentor who can help you see yourself for who you *could* be, not who you currently are. And then use that image to inspire you to start stretching.

4. Stretching Always Requires Change

Growth doesn't come from staying in your comfort zone. You can't improve and avoid change at the same time. So how do you embrace change and kick yourself out of your comfort zone?

First of all, stop looking over your shoulder. It's difficult to focus on your past and change in the present. That's why for years I had on my desk a little plaque that said, "Yesterday ended last night." It helped me to focus on the present and work to improve what I could *today*. That's important.

Second, if you want to grow and change, you must take risks. Innovation and progress are often initiated by people who push for change. It's unfortunate that the word *entrepreneur* has come to mean *gambler* to some people. But risk has advantages. People who take risks learn more and faster than those who don't. Their depth and range of experience is often greater. And they learn how to solve problems. All of these things help a person to grow.

The greatest stretching seasons of life come when we do what we have never done, push ourselves harder, and reach in a way that is uncomfortable to us. That takes courage. But the good news is that it causes us to grow in ways we thought were impossible.

5. Stretching Sets You Apart from Others

America seems to be increasingly satisfied with mediocrity. Yet it isn't at its root a national problem; it's a personal concession to do less than our best. It takes an individual to say, "I guess good enough is good enough." But unfortunately, mediocrity spreads from person to person and eventually metastasizes until an entire nation is at risk.

Excellence seems to be moving farther and farther from the norm. However, people who focus on stretching and use the tension between where they are and where they could be as impetus to stretch can distinguish themselves from their peers.

Improving yourself is the best way to help your team, your community, and your family. Successful people set themselves apart because they initiate the improvement others need. When you get better, those around you benefit. Excellence has the potential to spread in the same way that mediocrity does. The positives or negatives of a group always begin with one. When you get better, so will others.

6. Stretching Can Become a Lifestyle

When we stop stretching, I believe we stop really living. We may keep on breathing. Our vital life signs may be working. But we are dead on the inside and dead to our greatest possibilities. I'm getting older. I will not always be able to perform at my peak level. But I intend to keep reading, asking questions, talking to interesting people, working hard, and exposing myself to new experiences until I die. Too many people are dead but just haven't made it official yet!

I'm going to keep on stretching until I'm all stretched out. And it doesn't matter whether I see success today or not. Why? Because, sadly, many people stop growing after they have tasted success. I don't want success, no matter how great or small, to derail me.

7. Stretching Gives You a Shot at Significance

Indian statesman Mahatma Gandhi stated, "The difference between what we do and what we are capable of doing would suffice to solve most of the world's problems." That difference is the gap between good and great. And what closes the gap is our willingness to stretch.

People who exist on the "good" side of the gap live in the land of the permissible. What they do is okay. They follow the rules and don't make waves. But do they make the difference they could if they learned to focus on stretching? Cross over the gap and you find yourself on the "great" side. That is the land of the possible. It's where people achieve in extraordinary fashion. They do more than they believed they were capable of, and they make an impact. How? By continually focusing on making the next stretch. They continually leave their comfort zone and stretch toward their capacity zone.

We may appreciate what we did yesterday, but we should never put it on a pedestal. It should look small in comparison to the possibilities in the future. Looking forward fills us with energy. We resonate with the words of Robert Louis Stevenson, who said, "To be what we are, and to become what we are capable of becoming, is the only end in life."

Significance can be birthed within each of us. If we are

willing to stretch, that seed can grow until it begins to bear fruit in our lives. What's fantastic is that the change within us challenges us to make changes around us, and our growth creates a belief in us that others can grow. When that happens in a positive environment and everybody is stretching and growing, then indifference is replaced with make-a-difference. And that's how we begin to change our world.

How to Get Used to Stretching Yourself

1. In what areas of your life have you lost your stretch and settled in? Wherever they are, you need to find internal reasons to seek the tension to stretch again. Tap into your internal discontent to get you going. Where are you falling short of your potential? What goals haven't you hit that you know you're capable of? What habits have you developed that are hindering you from moving forward? What areas of past success have you stopped winning in? Remember, change is the key to growth. Use your lack of satisfaction to get you started anyplace you've stalled.

2. Be strategic to maintain the tension between where you are and where you could be by continually resetting intermediate-range goals for yourself. If goals are too immediate, you lose the tension when you achieve them quickly. If the goals are too lofty, they can seem too difficult to achieve and become discouraging.

What is the right time frame for you to maintain the tension? Three months? Six months? A year? Set goals for yourself according to your individual personality, and then keep revisiting them at the end of those time increments. You want the goal to be just barely within reach—not too easy, but not impossible either. Being able to figure this out is an art. But it will pay tremendous dividends in your life.

3. If you need an overarching goal to keep you stretching, think about what significant action you could take if only you become what you could be. Dream big, and set this as your lifetime goal.

11

Make Smart Trade-Offs

You Have to Give Up to Grow Up

What will it take for you to go to the next level? Vision? Yes. Hard work? Of course. Personal growth? Definitely. How about letting go of some of the things that you love and value most? Yes, and believe it or not, this is the thing that often holds people back, even those who have achieved some level of success.

When you're first starting out in your career it's not very hard to give up to grow up. In fact, you're willing to give up everything for an opportunity. Why? Because your "everything" isn't much of anything! But what about when you've started to earn some things: a job you enjoy, a good salary, a home, a community you've become a part of, a level of security? Are you willing to give up those things for a *chance* at doing something that will take you closer to your potential?

The Truth About Trade-Offs

Life has many intersections, opportunities to go up or down. At these intersections we make choices. We can add something to our life, subtract from it, or exchange something we have for something we don't. The most successful people know when to do which one of those three. Here are some insights that I hope will help you to understand trade-offs, spot them, and use them to your advantage.

Trade-Offs Are Available to Us Throughout Life

Everybody makes trades throughout life, whether they know it or not. The question is whether you are going to make good ones or bad ones. In general, I believe that...

> Unsuccessful people make bad trade-offs.
> Average people make few trade-offs.
> Successful people make good trade-offs.

You have to be willing to keep making significant trade-offs if you want to keep growing and striving to reach your potential. When you stop making them, you will arrive at a dead end in life. And at that point your growth will be done. And that will be the day that your best years are behind you and your potential is no longer ahead of you.

We Must Learn to See Trade-Offs as Opportunities for Growth

Nothing creates a greater gap between successful and unsuccessful people than the choices we make. Too often, people make life more difficult for themselves because they make bad choices at the intersections of their life or they decline to make choices because of fear. But it's important to remember that while we don't always get what we want, we always get what we choose.

Whenever I face an opportunity for a trade-off, I ask myself two questions:

WHAT ARE THE PLUSES AND MINUSES OF THIS TRADE-OFF?

Anytime you react to one of life's crossroads according to fear rather than looking at its merits, you close yourself off from a potential opportunity. Figuring out the pluses and minuses of any given choice helps you deal with that fear. Looking at cold, hard facts can also lead you to discover that you have a tendency to overestimate the value of what you currently have and underestimate the value of what you may gain by giving it up.

WILL I *GO* THROUGH THIS CHANGE OR *GROW* THROUGH THIS CHANGE?

Good trade-offs are not something to be endured. That reflects a passive attitude and a mind-set that says, "I hope this turns out all right." Instead, positive trade-offs should be seen as opportunities for growth and seized. After all, we become better as a result of them. When we grow through change, we become active. We take control of our attitude and emotions. We become positive-change agents in our own lives.

Years ago I determined that while others may lead timid lives, I would not. While others might see themselves as victims, I would not. While others leave their future in someone else's hands, I will not. While others simply *go* through life, I will *grow* through it. That is my choice, and I will surrender it to no one.

Trade-Offs Force Us to Make Difficult Personal Changes

The difference between where we are and where we want to be is created by the changes we are willing to make in our lives. When you want something you have never had, you must do something you've never done to get it. Otherwise you keep getting the same results. Changes to our lives always begin with changes we are willing to make personally. That's often not easy. But to get ourselves over the hump, we need to remember that...

Change is Personal—To change your life, *you* need to change.

Change is Possible—Everyone *can* change, including you.

Change is Profitable—You will be rewarded when you *do* change.

Change may not always be easy, but it can always be done. We just need to remember that we are the key.

The Loss of a Trade-Off Is Usually Felt Long Before the Gain

Sometimes we want a change, but we don't want to wait for the result. And often we become acutely aware of what we have lost in the trade because we feel that immediately, while we often don't reap the benefit of the trade until days, weeks, months, years, or even decades later. These in-between periods of transition can be a real challenge. We want the outcome, but we have to face the end of something we like and face the uncertainty between that ending and the hoped-for new beginning. The change feels like a loss.

Some people deal with uncertainty fairly well; others don't. Some recover from the psychological stress of change fairly quickly and process through it successfully; others don't. How well you do will depend partly on personality and partly on attitude. You can't change your personality, but you can choose to have a positive attitude and focus on the upcoming benefits of the trade-off.

Most Trade-Offs Can Be Made at Any Time

There are many trade-offs in life that can be made at any time. For example, we can give up bad habits to acquire good ones anytime we have the willpower to make the decision. Getting an appropriate amount of sleep, trading inactivity for exercise, and developing better eating habits to improve our health are all matters of choice, not opportunity. Obviously, the sooner we make such decisions the better, but most of the time they are not time driven.

After they make a bad trade-off, people often panic, feeling that they have blown it and can never recover. But seldom is that true. Most of the time, we can make choices that will help us to come back. So when it comes to choices, never say never. Never is a long, undependable thing and life is too full of rich possibilities to have that kind of restriction placed on it.

A Few Trade-Offs Come Only Once

The cycle of change gives us windows of opportunity in which to make decisions. Sometimes that cycle only goes around once. Miss it and the opportunity is gone.

The Higher You Climb, the Tougher the Trade-Offs

As you climb and accumulate some of the good things of life, the trade-offs demand a higher price. When we're at the bottom, we make trade-offs because of desperation. We are highly motivated to change. As we climb, we change because of inspiration. At this higher level we don't have to anymore. We get comfortable. As a result, we don't make the trade-offs.

One of the dangers of success is that it can make a person unteachable. Many people are tempted to use their success as permission to discontinue their growth. They become convinced that they know enough to succeed and they begin to coast. "You can't argue with success," they say. But they're wrong because the skills that got you *here* are probably not the skills that will get you *there*. If you want to keep growing and learning, you need to keep making trades. And they will cost you.

In the end, when we make trades we are trading one part of ourselves for another part. You give part of your life to receive something back. That may not be easy, but it's essential.

Trade-Offs Never Leave Us the Same

We all have the power of choice, but every time we make a choice, our choice has power over us. It changes us. Even the bad choices can ultimately help us to change for good, because they clarify our thinking and show us ourselves.

Some Trade-Offs Are Never Worth the Price

I'm all for making trade-offs. I have come to see it as a way of life. But not everything in my life is on the trading block. I'm not willing to trade my marriage for my career. I'm not willing to trade my relationship with my children or grandchildren for fame or fortune. And I'm not willing to trade away my values for anything or anyone. These kinds of trade-offs only lead to regret. And they are difficult to recover from.

I believe that most people who make these kinds of devastating trades don't realize they're making them until after it's too late. That's why I believe it's important to create systems and draw lines to keep ourselves safe. For example, I give Margaret veto power over my schedule to keep me from spending too much time working. I also avoid being alone with any women other than family members. And I spend time every day in prayer to keep my values front and center in my life. I highly recommend that you make choices and use systems to keep yourself grounded and on track.

Trade-Offs Worth Making

What kinds of trade-offs have you been making so far in your life? Have you thought about it? Have you developed guidelines to help you decide what to strive for and what to give up in return? Allow me to give you five trade-offs that I have thought through that may help you to develop your own guidelines:

1. I Am Willing to Give Up Financial Security Today for Potential Tomorrow

Physician and writer George W. Crane said, "There is no future in any job. The future lies in the man who holds the job." I have always believed that to be true, and as a result,

I have always been willing to bet on myself, so much so that I often accepted financial risks or pay cuts to pursue what I believed was a good opportunity.

2. I Am Willing to Give Up Immediate Gratification for Personal Growth

When it comes to growth and success, immediate gratification is almost always the enemy of growth. We can choose to please ourselves and plateau, or we can delay our gratification and grow. It's our choice.

3. I Am Willing to Give Up the Fast Life for the Good Life

We live in a culture that idolizes movie and music stars, drools over opulent mansions, idealizes travel, and plays the lottery in hopes of someday getting the chance to live the fast life it so admires and emulates. But most of that is an illusion. It's like the airbrushed image of a model on the front of a magazine. It's not real. That's just one of the reasons I choose to forgo the fast life in favor of the good life. If you do the right work with purpose in the right place with people you love, you will be living the good life.

4. I Am Willing to Give Up Security for Significance

I know many people whose goal in life is security: emotional security, physical security, and financial security. But I don't think it's wise to measure progress according to security. I think it's wiser to measure it by significance. And that requires growth. You'll never get anywhere interesting by always doing the safe thing. Every trade-off is a challenge to become what we really are. Managed correctly, trade-offs can create opportunities to help others become who they really are. That is significance!

5. I Am Willing to Give Up Addition for Multiplication

I started my career as an achiever. My attitude in the beginning was, "What can I do for others?" But that is addition. Once I began to learn leadership, my question changed to, "What can I do *with* others?" That's multiplication.

If you do not already consider yourself a leader, I want to encourage you to explore developing your leadership potential. However, if you believe that you don't have it in you to lead others, then consider becoming a mentor. Your investment in others will have a multiplying effect, and you won't regret the time you give.

Most people try to take too many things with them as they journey through life. They want to keep adding without giving anything up. It doesn't work. You can't do everything; there is only so much time in a day. At some point, you reach your limit. Besides, we need to always remember that if nothing changes, nothing changes!

How to Make Smart Trade-Offs

1. Write your own personal list of trade-off principles. Start by using the list in the chapter to spark ideas:

- I Am Willing to Give Up Financial Security Today for Potential Tomorrow
- I Am Willing to Give Up Immediate Gratification for Personal Growth
- I Am Willing to Give Up the Fast Life for the Good Life
- I Am Willing to Give Up Security for Significance
- I Am Willing to Give Up Addition for Multiplication

Think about worthwhile trade-offs you have made in the past that you believe will continue to be good ideas for the future. Also consider what might be needed for you to reach your potential along with what you might need to give up to fulfill it.

2. It's just as important for you to know what you *are not willing* to give up as it is to identify what you *are willing* to give up. Think through the things that are nonnegotiable in your life and list them. Then for each, identify its greatest potential threat and what safety measures you need to put into place to protect it.

3. What trade do you need to make right now that you have been unwilling to make? Most people settle in and learn to live with a limitation or barrier that can be removed by making a trade. What is that next thing you need to trade for? And what must you give up to get it?

12

Learn to Ask More Questions
Growth Is Stimulated by Asking Why?

I believe curiosity is the key to being a lifelong learner, and if you want to keep growing and developing, you must keep on learning. Curious people possess a thirst for knowledge. They are interested in life, people, ideas, experiences, and events, and they live in a constant state of wanting to learn more. They continually ask *why?* Curiosity is the primary catalyst for self-motivated learning. People who remain curious don't need to be encouraged to ask questions or explore. They just do it—all the time. And they keep doing it. They know that the trail to discovery is just as exciting as the discoveries themselves, because there are wonderful things to be learned along the way.

How to Cultivate Curiosity

I often wonder why more people aren't curious. So many people seem to be indifferent. Why don't they ask *why?* Are some people simply born without the desire to learn? Are some people just mentally lazy? Or does life become so routine for some people that they don't mind living in a rut, doing the same things day in and day out? Can such people "wake up" their minds and become more curious so growth becomes more natural to them?

I believe so, which is why I recommend the following ten suggestions for cultivating curiosity:

1. Believe You Can Be Curious

Many people fill their minds with limiting beliefs. Their lack of personal confidence or self-esteem causes them to create barriers for themselves and put limitations on how and what they think. The result? They fail to reach their potential—not because they lack capacity but because they are unwilling to expand their beliefs and break new ground. We cannot perform outwardly in a way that is inconsistent with how we think inwardly. You cannot be what you believe you aren't. But here's the good news: You can change your thinking and as a result, your life.

Give yourself permission to be curious. The single greatest difference between curious, growing people and those who aren't is the belief that they *can* learn, grow, and change. As I explained in the chapter on becoming an intentional learner, you must go after growth. Knowledge, understanding, and wisdom will not seek you out. You must go out and acquire it. The best way to do that is to remain curious.

2. Have a Beginner's Mind-Set

The way you approach life and learning has nothing to do with your age. It has everything to do with your attitude. Having a beginner's mind-set means wondering why and asking a lot of questions until you get answers. It also means being open and vulnerable. If your attitude is like that of a beginner, you have no image to uphold and your desire to learn more is stronger than the desire to look good. You aren't as influenced by preset rules or so-called acceptable thinking.

People with a beginner's mind-set approach life the way that a child does: with curiosity.

The direct opposite of people who have a beginner's mind-set are the know-it-alls. They see themselves as experts. They have a lot of knowledge, education, and experience, so instead of asking why and starting to listen, they start talking and give answers. Anytime a person is answering more than asking, you can be sure they've slowed down in their growth and have lost the fire for personal growth.

3. Make Why *Your Favorite Word*

Albert Einstein said, "The important thing is not to stop questioning. Curiosity has its own reason for existing. One cannot help but be in awe when he contemplates the mysteries of eternity, of life, of the marvelous structure of reality. It is enough if one tries merely to comprehend a little of this mystery every day. Never lose a holy curiosity." The secret to maintaining that "holy curiosity" is to always keep asking why.

Most of the time, focused questions begin with the word *why*. That word can really help you to clarify an issue. And it's important how you ask the question. People with a victim's mind-set ask, "Why me?" Not because they want to know, but because they feel sorry for themselves. Curious people ask the question to find solutions so they can keep moving forward and making progress.

Ask why. Explore. Evaluate what you discover. Repeat. That's a pretty good formula for growth. Never forget, anyone who knows all the answers is not asking the right questions.

4. Spend Time with Other Curious People

When you think of curiosity, growth, and learning, do you think of formal education? I think in the early grades curiosity is encouraged, but after that, it's not. Most formal education steers people toward answers rather than questions. If you went to college, how many times did you hear a professor ask students to hold their questions until later so he could get through his notes or complete the syllabus? The emphasis is often on information over inquiry. Do you find an attitude of openness and inquiry in the corporate world instead? Usually not. Most corporations don't try to stimulate curiosity either.

So what must you do to cultivate curiosity and stimulate growth? You must seek out other curious people. Curiosity is contagious. I know of few better ways of cultivating and sustaining curiosity than being around others who possess great curiosity.

5. Learn Something New Every Day

One of the best ways to remain curious is to begin each day with a determination to learn something new, experience something different, or meet someone you don't already know. Doing this requires three things. First, you must wake up with an attitude of openness to something new. You must see the day as having multiple opportunities to learn.

Second, you must keep your eyes and ears open as you go through the day. Most unsuccessful people accept their day, tuning things out, simply hoping to endure it. Most successful people seize their day, focusing in, ignoring distractions. Growing people remain focused, yet maintain a sensitivity and awareness that opens them up to new experiences.

The third component is reflection. It does little good to see something new without taking time to think about it. It does no good to hear something new without applying it. I've found that the best way to learn something new is to take time at the end of the day to ask yourself questions that prompt you to think about what you learned. Remember, experience is not the best teacher; evaluated experience is.

6. Partake in the Fruit of Failure

A curious, growing person approaches failure differently than someone who isn't curious. Most people see failure, mistakes, and errors as signs of weakness. When they fail, they say, "I'll never do *that* again!" But people who grow and develop see failure as a sign of progress. They know that it is impossible to continually try without sometimes failing. It's part of the curiosity journey. Therefore, they make failure their friend.

When failure is your friend, you don't ask, "How can I distance myself from this experience?" Instead, you ask, "Why did this happen? What can I learn? How can I grow from this?" As a result, you fail fast, learn fast, and get to try again fast. That leads to growth and future success.

7. Stop Looking for the Right Answer

There are many people who are motivated to find *the* right answer to any question. But there is always more than one solution to a problem. If you believe there is only a single right solution, you either get frustrated because you can't find it, or if you think you have found it, you stop searching and perhaps miss better ideas. In addition, when you land on what you consider to be *the* right answer, you become complacent. No idea is perfect. No matter how good it is, it can always be improved.

If you want to avoid growing too comfortable and becoming stagnant, then keep asking questions and challenging the process. Keep asking if there is a better way to do things. Will that annoy complacent and lazy people? Yes. Will it energize, challenge, and inspire growing people? Yes!

8. Get Over Yourself

If you're going to ask questions and allow yourself to fail, then you will at times look foolish. Most people don't like that. Do you know what my response is? Get over yourself! We need to be more like young children, who don't worry if a question is foolish. They just ask it. They don't worry about whether they will look dumb trying something new. They just do it. And as a result, they learn.

9. Get Out of the Box

Most revolutionary ideas were disruptive violations of existing rules. They upset the old order. Most in-the-box thinkers possess a scarcity mind-set. They don't think there are many resources to go around. They believe they can't. The best way to make a sluggish mind active is to disturb its routine. Getting outside the box does that for a person.

10. Enjoy Your Life

Perhaps the greatest way to remain curious and keep growing is to enjoy life. That means taking risks—sometimes failing, sometimes succeeding, but always learning. When you enjoy your life, the lines between work and play begin to blur. We do what we love and love what we do. Everything becomes a learning experience.

When you're curious, the entire world opens up to you and there are few limits on what you can learn and how you can develop.

How to Learn to Ask More Questions

1. Think about the three to five major areas in your life where you focus most of your time and energy. How do you see yourself in each of those areas? Do you think of yourself as an expert or a beginner? If you see yourself as an expert, you may be in trouble when it comes to further growth. Beginners know they have a lot to learn and are open to every possible idea. They are willing to think outside of the box. They don't get hung up on preconceived notions. They are willing to try new things.

If you have a beginner's mind-set in an area, do everything you can to maintain it. If you have come to think of yourself as an expert, beware! Find a way to rekindle a learner's attitude. Find a mentor who is ahead of you in that area. Or look for the fun again.

2. Make a list of the people you spend the most time with in a given week. Now rate each person on his or her level of curiosity. Are the majority of people in your world questioners? Do they often ask why? Do they like to learn new things? If not, you need to make some intentional changes to spend time with more curious people.

3. One of the greatest obstacles to curiosity and learning is the reluctance to look foolish in the eyes of other people. There are two indications that this may be a potential problem

in your life: The first is being afraid to fail. The second is taking yourself too seriously.

The cure is to take what I call "learning risks." Sign up to do or learn something that takes you completely out of your comfort zone. Take an art class. Sign up for dance lessons. Study a martial art. Learn a foreign language. Find a master at calligraphy or bonsai to train you. Just be certain to pick something that you find fun, where you cannot be seen as an expert, and that is far out of your comfort zone.

13

Find a Good Mentor

It's Hard to Improve When You Have No One but Yourself to Follow

I have learned a lot from people I've never met. Dale Carnegie taught me people skills when I read *How to Win Friends and Influence People* in junior high school. James Allen helped me understand that my attitude and the way that I thought would impact the course of my life when I read *As a Man Thinketh*. And Oswald Sanders revealed the importance of leadership to me for the first time when I read his book *Spiritual Leadership*. Most people who decide to grow personally find their first mentors in the pages of books. That is a great place to start. For that matter, it's a great place to continue. Every year I learn from dozens of people whom I will never meet. But at some point, you must find personal models too. If you follow only yourself, you will find yourself going in circles.

But you must be selective in whom you choose as a mentor. From both the positive and the negative experiences I've had with mentors, I have developed criteria to determine the "worthiness" of a model for me to follow. I share them with you in the hope that they will help you to make good choices for this area of your growth.

1. A Good Mentor Is a Worthy Example

We become like the people we admire and the models we follow. For that reason, we should take great care when determining which people we ask to mentor us. They must not only display professional excellence and possess skill sets from which we can learn, they must also demonstrate character worthy of emulating.

Many athletes, celebrities, politicians, and business leaders today try to disavow being any kind of role model when others are already following them and mimicking their behavior. They want people to separate their personal behavior from their professional life, but such a division cannot really be made. As you look for role models and mentors, scrutinize their personal lives as carefully as their public performance. Your values will be influenced by theirs, so you shouldn't be too casual about whom you choose to follow.

2. A Good Mentor Is Available

For us to be able to observe models up close and see what they do, we must have some contact with them. That requires access and availability. For us to be actively mentored, we must have time with people to ask questions and learn from their answers.

The greatest piece of advice I can give in the area of availability is that when you are looking for a mentor, don't shoot too high too soon. If you're considering going into politics for the first time, you don't need the advice of the president of the United States. If you are a high school student thinking about learning to play the cello, you don't need to be mentored by Yo-Yo Ma. If you're fresh out of school and just starting your career, don't expect to get extensive mentoring time from the CEO of your organization.

Why shouldn't I? you may be thinking. *Why not start with the best?* First of all, if you're just starting out, nearly all of your questions can be answered by someone two or three levels ahead of you (not ten). And their answers will be fresh because they will have recently dealt with the issues you're dealing with. Second, CEOs need to be spending their time answering the questions of the people who are on the verge of leading at their level. I'm not saying you should never go to the top. I'm saying spend the majority of your time being mentored by people who are available, willing, and suited for the stage of your career. And as you progress in your development, find new mentors for your new level of growth.

3. A Good Mentor Has Proven Experience

The farther you go in the pursuit of your potential, the more new ground you will have to break. How do you figure out how to proceed? Benefit from others' experience. As the Chinese proverb says, "To know the road ahead, ask those coming back." I don't know of a successful person who hasn't learned from more experienced people. Sometimes they follow in their footsteps. Other times they use their advice to help them break new ground.

4. A Good Mentor Possesses Wisdom

The understanding, experience, and knowledge of mentors with wisdom help us to solve problems that we would have a hard time handling on our own. Wise people often use just a few words to help us learn and develop. They open our eyes to worlds we might not have otherwise seen without their help. They help us navigate difficult situations. They help us to see opportunities we would otherwise miss. They make us wiser than our years and experience.

5. A Good Mentor Provides Friendship and Support

The first question most followers ask of a mentor is, "Do you care for me?" The reason for this question is obvious. Who wants to be guided by a person who isn't interested in them? Selfish people will assist you only insofar as it advances their own agenda. Good mentors provide friendship and support, unselfishly working to help you reach your potential.

If the person who offers to mentor you doesn't really support you and offer you friendship, then the relationship will always fall short of your expectations. Knowledge without support is sterile. Advice without friendship feels cold. Candor without care is harsh. However, when you are being helped by someone who cares for you it is emotionally satisfying. Growth comes from both the head and the heart. Only supportive people are willing to share both with you.

6. A Good Mentor Is a Coach Who Makes a Difference in People's Lives

Coaches make a difference in others' lives. They help them grow. They improve their potential. They increase their productivity. They are essential to helping people effect positive change.

In my opinion, good coaches share five common characteristics. They...

- **C**are for the people they coach
- **O**bserve their attitudes, behavior, and performance
- **A**lign them with their strengths for peak performance
- **C**ommunicate and give feedback about their performance
- **H**elp them to improve their lives and performance

The process of growing with the help of a mentor usually follows this pattern: It begins with awareness. You realize that you need help and that following yourself is not a viable option for effective personal growth. When a person comes to such a realization, one of two things can happen. The first is that the person's pride swells up and he cannot bring himself to ask another person for advice. This is a common reaction. The other reaction to awareness is to humble yourself and say, "I need your help." That decision not only leads to greater knowledge, but it also often develops maturity. It reinforces that people need one another—not just when they're young and starting out, but their entire lives.

*   *   *

As I look back over my life, I recognize that the greatest assets to my growth journey were people. But then again, so were the greatest liabilities. The people you follow, the models you emulate, the mentors you take advice from help to shape you. If you spend your time with people who subtract from you, who belittle you or undervalue you, then every step forward that you attempt to take will be difficult. But if you find wise leaders, good role models, and positive friends, you will find that they speed you on your journey.

No matter who you are, what you have accomplished, how low or how high your life has taken you, you can benefit from having a mentor. If you've never had one, you have no idea how much it can improve your life. If you have had mentors, then you already know—and you should start passing it on by becoming a mentor to others, because you know that it's hard to improve when you have no one but yourself to follow.

How to Find a Good Mentor

1. Find a next-step mentor. Think about where you are currently in your career and the direction you would like to go. Look for someone you admire who is two or three steps ahead of you on that same track. This person doesn't necessarily need to be in your organization. Look for the qualities needed in a good mentor: a worthy example, availability, proven experience, wisdom, willingness to be supportive, and coaching skills. If those are present in this individual, ask him or her to mentor you.

Before any meeting with a mentor, come prepared with three to five thoughtful questions, the answers to which will help you significantly. After you've met, work to apply what you've learned to your own situation. Don't ask for another meeting until you have done that. At your next meeting, begin the session by telling your mentor how you applied what you learned (or how you tried to apply it and failed, so you can learn what you did wrong). Then ask your new questions. Follow this pattern, and your mentor will be rewarded for his or her effort and will probably be glad to continue helping you.

2. We all need people who can help us sharpen specific strengths or navigate through certain problem areas. Whom do you talk to when you have questions related to career, marriage, parenting, spiritual growth, personal disciplines, hobbies, and

so on? No one person can answer all of these questions. You need to find several individual "consultants" to help you.

Spend some time making two lists. First, list the specific strengths or skills you want to improve to reach your potential. Second, list the specific problem areas where you feel the need for ongoing guidance. Begin looking for people with expertise in these particular areas and ask them if they would be willing to answer questions when you have them.

3. Do you have long-term models whom you observe, follow, and learn from, people who can give you advice regarding the big picture of your life and career? Or are you trying to improve while having no one but yourself to follow? If you haven't been asking others to help you on your journey, it's time to start. Most of us begin by looking for worthy models to follow by reading about them in books. Start there. But don't leave it at that. Look for people who will give you access to their lives.

As you look for models and mentors, I want to give you a word of caution. Oftentimes, people look good from far away, but when you get to know them, you discover qualities you don't admire. If that happens to you, please don't allow it to discourage you. There are plenty of people out there who have integrity and who are worthy to be respected and followed. Keep looking for them and you will find them.

14

Focus on Enlarging Your Potential

Growth Always Increases Your Capacity

Have you maxed out your capacity? Have you reached your full potential as a person? I believe that if you are reading this, the answer is no. If you're still breathing and you are of sound mind, then you have the potential to keep increasing your capacity.

How do you push toward your potential and keep increasing your capacity? You must change how you think and you must change your actions. By growing in these two key areas, you increase your capacity dramatically.

How to Increase Your Thinking Capacity

I've heard that most experts believe people typically use only 10 percent of their true potential. That statement is staggering! If that is true, then the average person has huge capacity for improvement. It's as if we possess hundreds of acres of possibilities but keep only half an acre under cultivation. So how do we tap into the unused 90 percent? The answer is found in changing how we think and what we do. Let's start by looking at how you need to think to increase your capacity.

1. Stop Thinking *More Work* and Start Thinking *What Works?*

Ask most people how they can increase their capacity and they'll tell you by working more. There's a problem with that solution. More work will not necessarily increase your capacity. More of the same usually results in more of the same, when what we actually want is better than what we have.

To figure out what works, ask yourself the following three questions:

> What am I required to do?
> What gives the greatest return?
> What gives me the greatest reward?

These questions will help you to focus your attention on what you must do, what you ought to do, and what you really want to do.

2. Stop Thinking *Can I?* and Start Thinking *How Can I?*

At first glance, the questions *Can I?* and *How can I?* may appear to be very similar. However, the reality is that they are worlds apart in terms of results. *Can I?* is a question filled with hesitation and doubt. It is a question that imposes limitations. If that is the question you regularly ask yourself, you're undermining your efforts before you even begin. How many people could have accomplished much in life but failed to try because they doubted and answered no to the question "Can I?"

When you ask yourself "How can I?" you give yourself a fighting chance to achieve something. The most common reason people don't overcome the odds is that they don't challenge themselves enough. They don't test their limits. They don't push their capacity. *How can I?* assumes there is a way. You just need to find it.

If you have spent time in a negative environment or you have experienced abuse in your life, you may find this thinking transition to be very difficult. If that describes you, then let me take a moment to encourage you and explain something. I'm asking you to shift from *Can I?* to *How can I?* when maybe you need to change your thinking from *I can't!* to *How can I?* I believe that if you've gotten this far in this book, then deep down you already believe that you can achieve things. I believe you can too. I believe God has put in *every* person the potential to grow, expand, and achieve. The first step in doing that is believing that you can. I believe in you!

As you get started, it may not look like you're making progress. That doesn't matter. Don't give up. You can change your thinking. You can believe in your potential. You can use failure as a resource to help you find the edge of your capacities. You can enlarge your potential every day by learning, growing, increasing your capacity.

3. Stop Thinking One Door and Start Thinking Many Doors

When it comes to growth, you don't want to stake your future on one "door." It may not open! It's much better to consider many possibilities and look for multiple answers to all of your questions. Think in terms of options.

As I have learned to think *many doors* and explore options, here is what I have learned:

- There is more than one way to do something successfully.
- The odds of arriving anywhere increase with creativity and adaptability.
- Movement with intentionality creates possibilities.
- Failures and setbacks can be great tools for learning.
- Knowing the future is difficult; controlling the future is impossible.
- Knowing today is essential; controlling today is possible.
- Success is a result of continued action filled with continual adjustments.

The greatest challenge you will ever face is that of expanding your mind. It's like crossing the great frontier. You must be willing to be a pioneer, to enter uncharted territory, to face the unknown, to conquer your own doubts and fears. But here's the good news. If you can change your thinking, you can change your life.

How to Increase Your Capacity for Action

If you want to expand your potential and therefore your capacity, you must first change your thinking. However, if you change *only* your thinking and you neglect to change your actions, you will fall far short of your potential. To start expanding your capacity, take the following three steps:

1. Stop Doing Only Those Things You Have Done Before and Start Doing Those Things You Could and Should Do

The first step toward success is becoming good at what you know how to do. But the more that you do what you know, the more you discover additional worthy things you *could* do. When this occurs, you have a decision to make. Will you continue doing what you have always done, or will you make the leap and try new things? Doing new things leads to innovation and new discoveries, and among those discoveries is the realization of things you *should* do on a consistent basis. If you do those, you will continue to grow and expand your potential. If you don't, you will plateau.

The process of expanding one's potential is ongoing. It ebbs and flows. Opportunities come and go. The standards we must set for ourselves are constantly changing. What we *could* do changes as we develop. What we *should* do also evolves. We must leave behind some old things to take on new ones. It can be difficult work, but if we are willing, our lives are changed.

2. Stop Doing What Is Expected and Start Doing More Than Is Expected

We live in a culture that awards trophies to people for simply showing up, regardless of their contribution. Because of that, many people think they are doing well if they just do what is expected of them. I don't believe that helps people reach their potential or expand their capacity. To distinguish yourself, get noticed, and advance your career, you need to do and be more.

You have to rise above average. You can do this by asking more of yourself than others ask, expecting more from yourself than others expect, believing more in yourself than others believe, doing more than others think you should have to do, giving more than others think you should give, and helping more than others think you should help.

Doing more than is expected does more than just separate you from your colleagues by earning you a reputation for performance. It also trains you to develop a habit for excellence. And that compounds over time. Continued excellence expands your capabilities and your potential.

3. Stop Doing Important Things Occasionally and Start Doing Important Things Daily

Have you ever heard the expression "Life is a great big canvas and you should throw all the paint on it that you can"? I like the intent and exuberance of those words, but I don't think that advice is very good—unless you want a mess. A better thought is to make your life a masterpiece, which requires much thought, a clear idea, and selection when it comes to what paint you put on the canvas. How do you do that? By doing the important things every day.

Advancing confidently in the direction of one's dreams means doing what is important every day. To do what's not important every day does nothing for you. It merely uses up your time. To do the right thing only occasionally does not lead to consistent growth and the expansion of your life. Both components are necessary. Daily growth leads to personal expansion.

You have the potential to keep making progress until the day you die—if you have the right attitude about growth. You need to believe what Rabbi Samuel M. Silver did. "The greatest of all miracles," he said, "is that we need not be tomorrow what we are today, but we can improve if we make use of the potentials implanted in us by God."

How to Focus on Enlarging Your Potential

1. Have you made the mental transition from *I Can't!* or *Can I?* to *How can I?* Test yourself. Do some dreaming. Then ask yourself,

> If I knew I could not fail, what would I attempt?
> If I had no limitations, what would I like to do?
> If finances were not an issue, what would I be doing with my life?

Take time and write your answers to those questions.

Now, look at your answers. What is your gut-level response to them? Do you look at them and think, *That's far-fetched? This is impossible. How outlandish!* Or do you look at them and think, *How can I do that? What must I do to make this happen? What will I have to trade to make this transition?* If it's the latter, you are mentally ready to expand your capacity. If it's the former, you still have work to do. Spend some time figuring out what's stopping you from believing you can make the changes necessary to expand your life.

2. Give yourself an effectiveness audit so you can be sure you are thinking *What works?* instead of *more work*. Go back through your calendar and to-do lists from the past four weeks. (By the way, if you aren't using some kind of system to plan your days, that's the first step you need to take.) Try to quantify the amount of time you spent on every action and

activity during those four weeks. Then think about how much time you believe each activity should have taken, and give yourself an efficiency rating from A+ to F. Now sort all the activities into categories.

Where do you see patterns? What's working? What isn't working? What are you doing too much of, either because you're not being efficient enough or because the activity is off purpose? What changes do you need to make? Use the criteria of *required*, *return*, or *reward* to help you make judgments on what needs to change.

3. Do you have a plan and system to make sure you are doing what's important daily? First, define what is essential to you on a daily basis. Once you've created your list, figure out how you will manage to follow through on each of those priorities every day so you stay on track and continue to expand your potential.

15

Help Others Reach Their Potential

Growing Yourself Enables You to Grow Others

It is my hope that this final chapter will inspire you to be all you can be so you can help others to be all they can be. You cannot give what you do not have. But if you have worked to learn or earn something, you have the ability to pass it on to others. If you keep growing and determine to help others reach their potential, you will have much to give other people and make a positive impact on your world.

Be a River, Not a Reservoir

How do you increase your chances of being able to help others and make a significant contribution in your lifetime? Think of yourself as a river instead of a reservoir. Most people who do make personal growth part of their lives do it to add value to themselves. They are like reservoirs that continually take in water but only to fill themselves up. In contrast, a river *flows*. Whatever water it receives, it gives away. That's the way we should be as we learn and grow. That requires an abundance mind-set—a belief that we will keep receiving. But as long as you are dedicated to personal growth, you will never experience scarcity and will always have much to give.

Making the Right Contribution Choices

Giving of your time, expertise, and resources without expecting anything in return is an unselfish act that makes the world a better place. We need more givers. When you focus more on the wants and needs of others, more of your own wants and needs are met. In contrast, when you choose to hoard what you have, rather than give, you become the center of your own lonely universe and you become less content, not more. As a result, you repel both people and potential blessings.

You can become a more generous and giving person, even if you already exhibit those qualities. However, to do that, you must be a growing and developing person. And you must be intentional in your efforts to add value to others. Here are some suggestions to help you cultivate an attitude of contribution:

1. Be Grateful

People who aren't grateful are not givers. They rarely think about others; they think only of themselves. Their days consist of looking for others to help them, give to them, serve them. And whenever others don't fulfill those expectations, they wonder why. Their selfishness keeps them from sowing and their ingratitude makes them wonder why they don't reap a harvest! How can you show gratitude? By daily pouring into others and passing on to them the things that will allow them to run far and achieve beyond what you have done.

2. Put People First

All the things of this world are temporary. People are what matter. Your career, hobbies, and other interests will die with you. People continue on. What you give to help others builds them up enough that they are able to give to others. It's a cycle that can continue on long after you're dead and gone. Treating others well not only benefits people, it also helps us navigate life better and puts us in a place where we can learn from others.

The measure of success is not the number of people who serve you, but the number of people you serve. When people are number one in your life, adding value to them becomes natural. You do it as a matter of lifestyle. You add value to people because you value people and you believe that they have value.

3. Don't Let Stuff Own You

No one should ever become a slave to his stuff. No one should make acquiring more just for the sake of having more his life's work. If you want to be in charge of your heart, don't allow possessions to take charge of you. The question is, "Do you own your stuff or does your stuff own you?" Contributors take the stuff they own and use it as an asset to make this world a better place to live. And they do this regardless of how much or how little they have.

4. Don't Let People Own You

When Margaret and I were newly married and I was starting my career, we had very few resources. Basically, we were scraping to get by. During that time, we became friends with a couple that was financially well off. Each Friday night, Jack and Helen would take us to a fine restaurant and buy our meal. It was the highlight of my week, since Margaret and I could not afford to eat there. Over a two-year period we received many wonderful benefits of this friendship, and we were very grateful.

After three years in that position, I got an offer to become the leader of a larger church. It was a tremendous opportunity with great advancement and potential. When I announced that I would be leaving to take it, Jack was not pleased. I'll never forget his words: "John, how can you leave after all that I have done for you?" It was in that moment that I realized Jack was starting to slowly own me. He was keeping score, and I had no idea!

It was a wake-up call. That was the day I made a choice. I would always try to give more than I received in relationships. And I would never keep score. I would be on the giving side of life whenever possible. Obviously I still receive from others. I am blessed beyond words for what others have done for me. But I didn't want to give away control of my life. It's hard to give yourself away when someone else owns you. I wanted to be able to value people with no strings attached. A giving life should be liberating to yourself and to those you help.

5. Define Success as Sowing, Not Reaping

Novelist Robert Louis Stevenson said, "I consider the success of my day based on the seeds I sow, not the harvest I reap." That should be the way we judge not only our days, but our entire lives. Unfortunately most people sow little and expect to reap a lot. Their focus is on payday.

If you are sowing only for quick returns in life, then you will usually be unhappy with the outcome and unable to keep giving and living while waiting. On the other hand, if you sow continually and abundantly, you can be sure that in due season there will be a harvest. Successful people know this and focus on sowing, knowing that reaping will eventually come. The process is automatic. If you live life with the intention of making a difference in others' lives, your life will be full, not empty.

6. Focus on Self-Development, Not Self-Fulfillment

What's the main difference between self-development and self-fulfillment? The motive. Self-fulfillment means doing what I enjoy most. Self-development means doing what I am talented and uniquely fit to do, and that becomes my responsibility. Chasing self-fulfillment is a bit like chasing happiness. It's an emotion that cannot be sustained. It relies too much on circumstances. It depends on a person's mood. In contrast, you can develop yourself regardless of how you feel, what circumstances you find yourself in, your financial situation, or the people around you.

7. Keep Growing to Keep Giving

Whenever people stop actively learning and growing, the clock has started ticking down to a time when they will no longer have anything left to give. If you want to keep giving, you have to keep growing.

Sometimes people stop learning because they become complacent. They believe they have grown enough, or they want only to make the most of what they already have in terms of skill and knowledge. That's when they start to plateau and then decline. They lose their innovative spirit. They begin to think about being efficient instead of breaking ground. They cut costs instead of investing in growth. Their vision becomes very limited. And instead of playing to win, they start playing not to lose.

We all love doing what we're good at, but being good at something requires us to keep our skills sharp. Less skill leads to less enthusiasm and eventually discontent. If we reach this stage, we start looking behind us, because that is where our best days are. We think about the good old days, the glory days. At that point, we're only a few short steps from obsolescence. Nobody wants to learn from a has-been. If you want to give until you've given all you have, you must keep growing until you can grow no more.

How to Help Others Reach Their Potential

1. What is your underlying desire in life: Is it self-fulfillment or self-development? Are your efforts designed to make you feel good? Or to make you be your best? Is your goal to be successful? Or to achieve significance? Are you trying to achieve so you can feel happy? Or are you trying to put yourself in a place to help others win?

These distinctions may seem subtle, but they really make a difference. Trying to feel fulfilled brings a never-ending restlessness because you will never be completely satisfied. Trying to develop yourself is a never-ending journey and will always inspire you, because every bit of progress is a victory; yet there will always be new challenges to excite and inspire you.

2. Make sure that no person owns you. Make a list of the key people in your life. Now think about each relationship and determine if you are mostly the giver, you are mostly the taker, or the relationship is even.

If you are primarily the taker, then you need to make adjustments so the other person doesn't have power over you. Make the effort to outgive the people in your life without keeping score. You can do this not only with your family and friends, but even with your employer. Make an effort to give more work than your organization pays you for. Not only will the people you work for and with value you, but you will add value to them. And if you have an opportunity to move on to bigger and better things, you will be able to do so knowing that you have always given your best.

3. I have one final application exercise for you in this book, and that is to put people first in your life. Write down your top three to seven goals and dreams. Now write down the names of the most important people in your life. Be honest with yourself. Which comes first? The people? Or your goals and dreams?

Make the decision to put others ahead of your own agenda. Put your family ahead of your own desires. Put the development of people at the workplace ahead of your own advancement. Serve others instead of yourself. Commit to it, and then invite others in your life to hold you accountable. And remember, sometimes the seeds you sow take a long time to grow. But there *always* is a harvest.

HOW SUCCESSFUL PEOPLE LEAD

Taking Your Influence to the Next Level

JOHN C. MAXWELL

True leadership is not generated by your title. In fact, being named to a position is the lowest of the five levels every effective leader achieves. To be more than a boss people are required to follow, you must master the ability to inspire and invest in people. You need to build a team that produces not only results, but also future leaders. By combining the advice contained in these pages with skill and dedication, you can reach the pinnacle of leadership—where your influence extends beyond your immediate reach for the benefit of others.

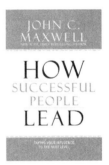

Available now from Center Street wherever books are sold.

CENTER STREET

Also available from **hachette** AUDIO **and** **hachette** DIGITAL

Change Your Thinking, Change Your Life
with John C. Maxwell's
Wall Street Journal best seller

HOW SUCCESSFUL PEOPLE THINK

Good thinkers are always in demand.
They solve problems, never lack ideas, and
always have hope for a better future. In this
compact read for today's fast-paced world,
Maxwell reveals eleven types of successful
thinking, and how you can maximize each
to revolutionize your work and life.

Also available from  and

And look for

HOW SUCCESSFUL PEOPLE THINK WORKBOOK

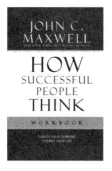

An interactive companion providing
overviews, case studies, questions,
exercises, and action steps for each type
of thinking that will help you apply
the principles learned in Maxwell's
pocket-sized triumph.

Available now from Center Street wherever books are sold.

CENTER
STREET

Free companion app available now for download

THE 15 INVALUABLE LAWS OF GROWTH

JOHN C. MAXWELL

Available on your iPhone and iPad, this free practical companion app will help you maximize the application of John C. Maxwell's Laws of Growth.

- Create and track the progress of your personal goals.
- Share quotes from the book with friends via Twitter and Facebook.
- Keep important thoughts front of mind in a dedicated Favorite Quotes place.
- Sample other editions of the book and check out other John Maxwell titles.

Also look for *The 5 Levels of Leadership* App.

CENTER
STREET